SUCCESSION MANAGEMENT

The Definite "Do's" and the Detrimental "Don'ts"

ASHNIE MUTHUSAMY

TALENT MANAGEMENT SERIES

First published in 2018.

ISBN: 978-1-86922-751-7
eISBN: 978-1-86922-752-4 (ePDF)

Published by KR Publishing
P O Box 3954
Randburg
2125
Republic of South Africa

Tel: (011) 706-6009
Fax: (011) 706-1127
E-mail: orders@knowres.co.za
Website: www.kr.co.za

Printed and bound: Tandym Print, 1 Park Road, Western Province Park, Epping, 7475
Typesetting, layout and design: Cia Joubert, cia@knowres.co.za
Cover design: Marlene de'Lorme, marlene@knowres.co.za
Editing and proofreading: Jennifer Renton, jenniferrenton@live.co.za
Illustrations: Robyn Shirley
Project management: Cia Joubert, cia@knowres.co.za

Table of Contents

About the Author

Ashnie Muthusamy is presently the Group Talent Manager for Sun International. She has a Honours Degree in Psychology, a Master's Diploma in HR Management and a Masters Degree in Leadership. She is a registered counsellor in Psychometry with the HPCSA. For the last 20 years she has taken on various group roles working in Talent Management. Her present portfolio includes Strategic Resourcing, Psychometric Assessment, Job Architecture, Performance Management, Succession Management and EVP, among other HR responsibilities.

Introduction

In the early 2000s I was appointed the Group Talent Manager for one of the established South African banking groups. Talent management as a concept had just swept up on the South African shore and whilst there had already been some work done overseas, in South Africa it was unchartered territory and considered very much "Greenfield". McKinsey had just published their famous article, *The War for Talent*, and all the South African organisations were focused on understanding the impact of the new paradigm shift.[1] The focus moved from organisations determining their terms and conditions, to employees who had suddenly discovered the freedom to sell their talent and capabilities to the highest bidding organisation.

It was in this ambiguous environment that I started my electrifying journey with succession management. As the practices developed and matured, so did my experience and knowledge. The best teacher is often experience, and I quickly learnt that I needed to find my own meaning in this discipline called talent management.

When the book *The Leadership Pipeline* was published in 2002, there was a figurative collective sigh amongst talent specialists who viewed it as a magical formula for grouping employees into different talent categories.[2] They understood that retaining talent was important but had little idea on how to proceed. Almost one and a half decades later, and the talent grid discussed in that book has become closely woven into the talent frameworks of many South African organisations.

Whilst this provided a great start, there was so much more to learn about talent management, and more specifically, succession management. This book is the product of my own personal knowledge and years of experience, and provides some of the foundational lessons that have shaped my view on succession, such as:

- ✓ Don't complicate the process with templates and documents. The essence of succession is often lost in the accumulation of content, and it is often difficult to wade through a sea of paper.

- ✓ Worry about technology and systems last; the communication, understanding and adoption of the process is the focal point.

- ✓ Identifying successors means little if there are no robust development interventions in place and if development is not tracked and monitored.

- ✓ Transformation is not an afterthought but an essential variable in the identification, development and transition of successors.

- ✓ Be sensitive to the emotional dynamics of succession and the psychological impact it has on all stakeholders.

- ✓ Succession is a long term process and often you may not be around to see the results of your efforts come to fruition, so get real time feedback through regular reviews of talent metrics.

- ✓ In succession you will never always be the "hero" but will often be cast as the villain, so have the maturity to never take it personally.

- ✓ Never underestimate organisational politics in succession; be able to recognise it when it plays out so that you can counteract or reduce the negative impact of it.

- ✓ Establish a level of competence and credibility with stakeholders so that they trust you to be objective in any situation.

- ✓ Play nicely with other HR functional specialists. The effectiveness of succession is highly dependent on the integration and support of other HR practices.

- ✓ Your greatest lessons often come not from success but from process failure. Use the opportunity to reflect on the variables that influenced the outcome. Remember these and mitigate for them in the future.

Thank you for choosing to travel this fascinating succession path with me. I am going to draw on a combination of my accumulated experience and lessons from renowned HR leaders and business executives that I have had the privilege to work with. They have passed the baton on to me through their mentorship and wisdom. It has not always been an easy ride but more of a rollercoaster that required high levels of patience, tenacity and resilience against unpredictable waves of resistance. My journey has been paved with opportunities for growth, significant challenges, complex yet colourful leadership characters, and well learned lessons that have provided a great foundation for what works and does not work effectively in succession.

Succession management is often viewed as an intense subject, so I have tried to lighten this book with snippets of real life stories. I have changed the details to provide anonymity to the individuals. The metaphoric writing style with both real and anecdotal stories aims to convey insight and keep you interested right until the end of our journey. Whilst I make references to experts and to other research, this in no way should be seen as a succession management text book in the conventional sense. There is also an inclusion of material from other subject areas that add credence to the different topics discussed. The approach in this guide to succession is thus more eclectic.

Every practice occurs within a context. Due to the interdependencies of succession with other HR practices, I will make brief references to those HR practices that are impacted by succession and influence the effectiveness of succession in organisations.

The misconception in organisations is that succession is easy. "Find suitable people who may replace future critical role vacancies and voilà you are doing succession." It is often one of the most underestimated practices. The challenge with this approach is that given the new context of the world of work and its various factors, the application of this approach may be plagued with inconsistencies, creating a culture of entitlement, disengaging other employees not on a succession list, and the succession plan may never be actioned due to the continuously changing business demands.

Who is this book for?

This book is intended for the HR Business Partner, Learning and Development Practitioner or Line Manager who is a novice to the world of talent management, and more especially succession management, i.e. this book is intended for HR business partners with a basic level of HR knowledge, experience and expertise who are working in organisations with different levels of business maturity. The intention is to provide broad guidelines on implementing succession management, taking cognisance of existing organisational culture, readiness and leadership maturity. Although the type of process and the extent of succession management may be different, organisations both large and small should have some form of succession plan. This book is not intended to be an exhaustive resource for succession management practices, but is aimed at providing basic concepts and processes for the HR practitioner to easily implement with confidence. I have also included references for some literature and a few websites that provide more depth into some of the concepts I cover.

I have made use of the two genders interchangeably in the book to prevent any perception of gender bias. In addition, I have included a generic succession process that you can adapt and customise based on your needs.

Using this book

This book follows the Succession Management Practice Flow Chart on page 7. There are three main sections which focus on all the necessary steps to introduce a new practice into an organisation.

Section one refers to the necessary preparation that happens in the organisation before implementing a succession process. This is covered in Chapters One to Five.

Section two focuses on implementing succession management and includes developing and designing the process as well as successfully managing the change. This is reviewed in Chapters Five to Seven.

Section three highlights the steps required to reinforce and embed succession as a sustainable practice. This is covered in Chapters Eight to Ten.

Each chapter starts with a short poem that provides a general introduction to the topic covered. This is followed by specific information that will assist in building a sustainable succession practice in your organisation. The chapters conclude with a summary of main hints and tips.

Through the text, you will find:

- quick tips: the 'do's' and 'don'ts' of succession;
- some suggestions for enhancing your process and improving your succession rollout; and
- anecdotal stories to illustrate certain messages and reinforce these ideas.

Flow chart for succession management

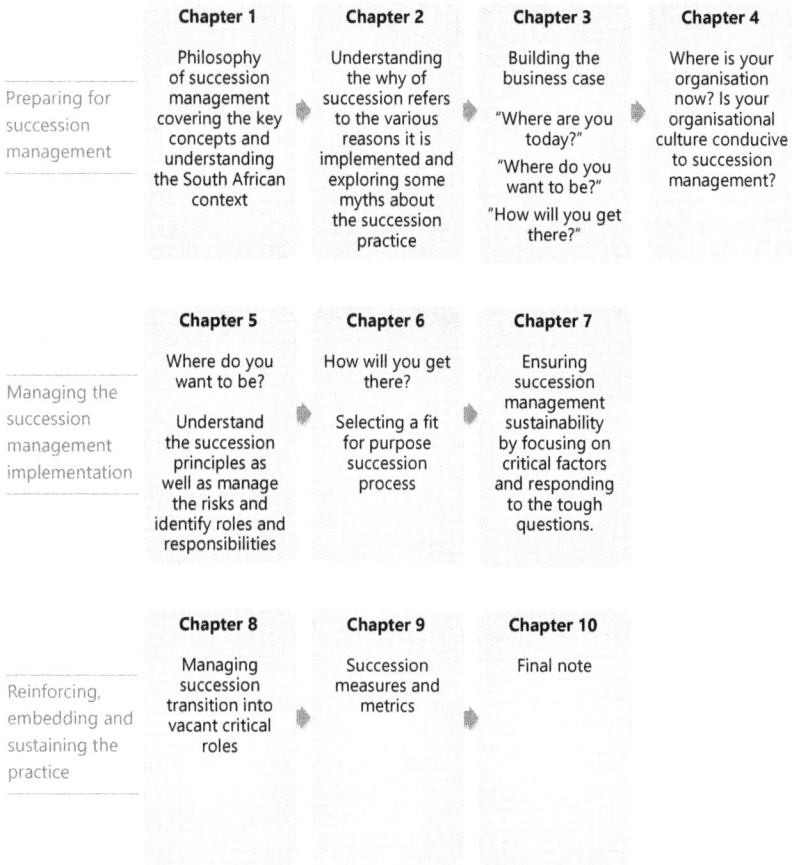

Preparing for succession management

Chapter 1	Chapter 2	Chapter 3	Chapter 4
Philosophy of succession management covering the key concepts and understanding the South African context	Understanding the why of succession refers to the various reasons it is implemented and exploring some myths about the succession practice	Building the business case "Where are you today?" "Where do you want to be?" "How will you get there?"	Where is your organisation now? Is your organisational culture conducive to succession management?

Managing the succession management implementation

Chapter 5	Chapter 6	Chapter 7
Where do you want to be? Understand the succession principles as well as manage the risks and identify roles and responsibilities	How will you get there? Selecting a fit for purpose succession process	Ensuring succession management sustainability by focusing on critical factors and responding to the tough questions.

Reinforcing, embedding and sustaining the practice

Chapter 8	Chapter 9	Chapter 10
Managing succession transition into vacant critical roles	Succession measures and metrics	Final note

Chapter 1

Philosophy of succession management

> *To equip you on this journey you need to grasp the basic succession concepts and views,*
>
> *Enabling you to navigate competently to become a succession management guru.*
>
> *Find out more about how the nature of succession changed over time,*
>
> *The shifting perspective from a secret to a transparent paradigm.*

The organisational view of succession management

Traditionally succession was done from an organisational perspective, where the focus was on maintaining business continuity; it was all about the organisational requirements and there was little consideration of employees' needs. For example, employees were identified as successors and placed on a succession plan, but were never informed. When the employee was ready to exit the organisation, only then were they told of the organisation's expectations. The result was that succession management was an unreliable form of long term business planning and was rarely actualised.

Imagine as an organisation that you have identified an employee on a succession plan because you think they have high potential and the required leadership competencies. However, you have never spoken to them about this opportunity and you have also not developed them in line with this role. When the time comes to transition the 'identified successor' into a new role, you meet and communicate the great news and opportunity. Instead of gratitude they meet you with a blank stare and let you know they are actually planning to follow their entrepreneurial dreams and open a new franchise business.

How could this scenario have worked out differently? You could have had a career conversation, identified their aspirations, and looked for an alternative successor whose career aspirations were aligned to the organisation, to mitigate this risk from happening.

---

tips/ideas

- Career conversations are a critical prerequisite to succession management.
- Build career conversations into the succession management process.

With the introduction of talent management practices there came a greater realisation that there needs to be a balance between organisational and individual needs. The focus shifted from the organisation dictating the terms and conditions that employees abided by to the sudden realisation that employees could choose jobs in various organisations, and in fact had the power to influence the terms and conditions of employment. This change of power also influenced how succession was done. There was a sudden consideration for the employee in the succession management process and career conversations become a pre-requisite for succession to align individual aspirations to organisational objectives.

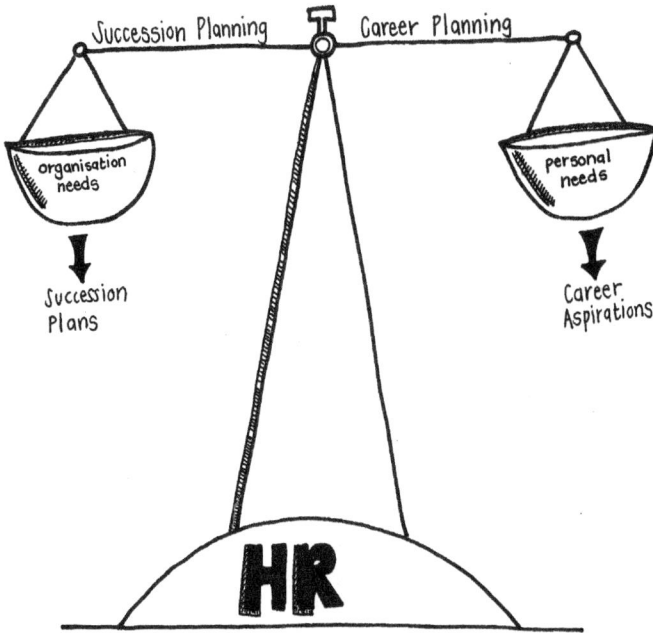

- balancing organisational and individual needs
  chapter 1

Succession Planning — Career Planning

organisation needs — personal needs

Succession Plans — Career Aspirations

HR

Balancing organisational and individual needs

Today, HR processes mediate the relationship between the employer and employee. A sustainable and integrated talent management approach includes both the individual's perspective (career management) and the employer's perspective (succession management). The individual's needs have to be considered in order to ensure there is perfect alignment between what employees want and what organisations need.

Succession management in South Africa

In South Africa, succession was traditionally a concept that was rarely discussed as it was underpinned by a code of confidentiality shared by a select few. The process of succession was usually never transparently communicated as it was often under the sole custodianship of the Chief Executive and his team, i.e. the participation of HR was often minimal. It was a decision based on a subjective perspective - often through gut feel - and about who deserved the honour, rather than a purely objective process based on job relevant competencies and potential. It was about tenure in the organisation and tenure in the role; loyalty and natural progression based on positional authority. For example, only the Group Financial Manager was the individual earmarked for the role of Chief Financial Officer. This approach gradually changed so that the pool of successors widened to other Group Executives as potential successors. This was the norm for many organisations in South Africa, yet succession practices have gradually changed to adapt to new business demands and the volatile business climate around the world.

The slow pace of diversity transformation in South African organisations is often a contentious topic in boardrooms. The inability to transition competent black people and women into senior roles is often blamed on organisations' poor succession management practices, thus it is a core principle that South African organisations have a corporate responsibility to transform. However many fall into the trap of poor policy, process and implementation, which undermines their good intentions and questions their commitment to real transformation. The larger social issues in South Africa permeate local organisations, where these social issues are often manifested in the workplace. There are certain threads of distrust, of stereotypes, and of racial, gender and other cognitive biases that colour people's perceptions of the potential and readiness of successors.

"A society grows great when old men plant trees whose shade they know they will never sit in."[3]

The above quote encompasses what the ultimate purpose of succession management should be in organisations, however the common practice is often that organisation-wide succession management is riddled with inconsistencies of application, and often relegated to being another practice that justifies favouritism covertly under the disguise of an objective process. The question often posed is how organisations should approach succession management in a transparent way that removes suspicion and doubt about the fairness of the process. The subsequent chapters will aim to answer this question.

Differentiating between succession planning and succession management

Having a common language allows people to communicate ideas more rapidly with less need for lengthy explanations. It is often said that words have power, and categorising apparently similar concepts into specific labels creates distinction and understanding. For this reason, the difference between succession planning and succession management needs to be explained.

Succession planning was a relevant practice when organisational change was predictable and the rate of turnover in organisations was manageable, with positions being occupied for long periods of time. Employees had long tenures in organisations and would follow career paths, so it was easier to plan around succession in a relatively stable environment.

The simplicity of succession planning is no longer relevant in the current context of a volatile, uncertain, complex and ambiguous world, however. What is required is a more sophisticated approach which incorporates continuous changing variables as applied with the concept of succession management.

Succession management is a robust and dynamic process that builds on the principles of succession planning and introduces other critical practices that define the continuous success of the process. The reality is that with innovation in business processes, technology transformation, the shifting legislative landscape, changing business imperatives and subsequent changes in job requirements, succession for an identified role is a moving target. Succession management introduces the concept of multiple options for identified roles and a holistic look at the leadership pool. This is the agile response to the concurrent challenges facing businesses today, and allows organisations to be prepared for a range of business challenges.

tips / ideas

Recognise the potential for succession management to transform your business from a diversity perspective.

Meaningful transformation is not about the numbers but about being authentic and creating an inclusive culture.

Recognise and manage the resistance to a transformation climate in the organisation, as this can derail succession objectives.

In transformation and succession, leadership alignment and commitment is integral to bringing about effective results.

The transfer of learning requires ongoing engagement, coaching and mentorship.

Succession focuses on building future business capabilities so a transformation mindset is not limited to the diversity of employees, but should extend to include the diversity of new business philosophies.

tips/ideas

The transition from succession planning to succession management		
Succession planning	**Progressed to**	**Succession management**
Moved from traditional replacement planning.	**Change in focus**	Moving towards a more relevant integrated succession management.
Successors were usually two individuals linked to a role.	**Number of successors**	Successors are usually a range of potential individuals from a talent pool and come from different areas of the business.
Organisational structures were more stable.	**Organisational structures**	The organisational structure is in a constant state of redesign.
Driven by annual HR procedures.	**Succession drivers**	Driven by future business strategy and needs.
Entitlement focused and held in secrecy.	**Identification of successors**	Succession is the result of multiple inputs and a greater level of consultation.
There were identified development actions but no accountability for development.	**Developmental focus**	There are specific individual development plans for successors and development is actioned and monitored.
Focused on senior roles only.	**Nature of successors**	Includes critical roles across levels in the organisation.

Employers did not share their succession plan with employees; the document was kept completely confidential.	**Level of transparency**	Employers share the succession plan with employees, with the understanding that there is no implicit guarantee of promotion without meeting developmental goals.
Focused primarily on the present; concerned with finding effective replacements for open positions.	**Time orientation**	Focuses on developing leaders for the future: identifying and building competencies to ensure that the leadership pipeline is maintained.
Employees were evaluated by means of traditional annual performance reviews; these assessments had little to do with developmental objectives.	**Continuous readiness assessment**	Individuals in the succession plans are reviewed frequently through 360-degree evaluations and leadership templates to assess progress relative to developmental goals.
Successors were identified purely on performance track record.	**Successor criteria**	Successors are identified for their potential to adapt easily and work with higher levels of complexity. Performance track record is one factor amongst many others.

The essence of succession management

Succession management is about acknowledging that employees will not stay in the organisation indefinitely and provides a realistic plan for when they leave. It is thus about proactively identifying key talent internally in a fair and systematic way in anticipation of future vacancies, and to prepare them by enhancing their potential through targeted developmental initiatives and support, thus enabling them to meet the minimum requirements for the next succession level.

The success of succession management lies in leadership buy-in and an objective fit for purpose strategy, process and plan. An objective fit for purpose strategy allows for transparency and thereby facilitates easy acceptance of the process, while a proper succession plan is a proactive, systematic effort designed to ensure the continued effective performance of an organisation, division, department and work group. The plan, meanwhile, provides for the development, replacement and strategic application of key people and processes over time. The key to succession management is continuity, i.e. the proper identification and placement of the right calibre people in the correct jobs to ensure that the strategic objectives of the organisation can be met in the short, medium and long term.

Having a succession plan only addresses 25% of the challenge; the other 75% is about legitimising the plan, implementing the plan, tracking and growing talent into ideal roles, reviewing the meeting of developmental goals, as well as monitoring the shifting organisational employee requirements to ensure future fit and suitability to roles.

Succession categories

When choosing a successor, there may be different potential successors for one role at different levels of readiness and development. The succession categories in Table 1 below are an example of some basic categories you can include in the succession template to define the level of readiness of possible successors to take up the designated roles. The volatility in your industry or business will determine the succession timeframes; a more stable business may have longer timeframes versus a more volatile business which constantly changes product lines and requires changing skill sets.

Table 1: Succession categories

emergency	**Emergency successors** should be those capable of doing the job for a short, cover period only - usually up to three months. This employee will be managing the portfolio or job until the position is filled by a suitable permanent employee. The role is often filled from several direct reports, a peer or someone of a similar level of seniority from another function. It can also be a person who has done this job successfully previously. If there are a few employees who can be emergency successors, they may rotated into the role. This provides a great developmental opportunity. Nominating an individual for whom the role would only be appropriate in three years is a high risk choice.
ready now	A **Ready Now** successor is a person who is presently competent and ready to take over the role immediately. This employee has all the relevant competencies and experience required to be successful in the role.
ready 1-2 years	**Ready 1 – 2 years** successors should be capable of potentially filling the role within this timeframe. It is important to understand what experience/development these employees require to be competent in the role. These employees usually have comprehensive individual development plans which target competencies that will be developed within specific timeframes. These development plans assist them to become fluent in the role.

ready 2 - 3 years	**Ready 2 – 3 years** successors should be capable of potentially filling the role within this timeframe. If there is a volatile environment with continuously changing business processes, the names in this column may be redundant if the position radically changes in the next two years. However, for organisations that are more or less constant, they can be included in the succession plan template.
none available	**None available** means there are no available successors for a role. This requires a business decision to either grow talent internally through graduate or designated programmes, or to externally source successors.
no longer neccessary	**No longer necessary** means that the job will cease to exist in the current form, or that it will be reengineered to include other responsibilities. Usually jobs merge or require a completely altered set of skills.

- Career conversations are a pre-requisite to succession to align individual aspirations to organisational objectives.

- Succession in South Africa is under a magnifying glass as organisations struggle to implement succession management (a transformation lever) successfully.

- Succession planning has evolved into succession management, which is a more integrated practice.

- Succession categories cover four main types: 'Emergency successors', 'Ready now successors', 'Ready 1 to 2 years' and 'Ready 2 to 3 years'.

Chapter 2

Understanding the why of succession management

> *Is there a burning platform for succession or is it a result of a whim?*
>
> *Who is the producer, director and cast in this succession management film?*
>
> *These profound questions often determine the sustainability and success of the process,*
>
> *As they define what will be the enablers and levers for succession progress.*

It is necessary to start by first framing why one undertakes succession before developing solutions. The rationale often creates a context which inspires people to take appropriate action.

Reflection exercise: A typical trigger for succession management

A hypothetical scenario

An email is sent from the Chief Executive's desk. It states that given the high level of turnover of senior positions in the organisation and the length to onboard new employees into these roles, succession has become imperative to address this business challenge. She asks that all Line Managers be supportive of the succession management process that HR will roll out.

The HR Director sees her email and reads this instruction for the first time along with the rest of the organisation. There is a mixture of anxiety and excitement, for it is a widely known fact that succession is a fundamental business process that has been discussed over the years, but there was never really any appetite from the executives who were in their mid-forties and saw it as an unnecessary bother.

Response one to the above scenario

The HR Director excitedly calls her team together and asks the talent specialist to quickly research a succession management guide that can be easily implemented. There is no time for questions, as a commitment has been made and HR credibility is on the line. She silences the queries from her team and steam rolls ahead. The HR Director stresses that speed of implementation is of the essence and non-delivery is not acceptable.

Response two to the above scenario

The HR Director quickly picks up her phone and calls a reputable HR consulting firm and asks them for a quote to implement succession management in the organisation. She stresses the urgency for the proposal so that the process can kick off. After receiving a quote, she asks the consultants to present at the next executive meeting on their implementation approach. She advises her HR team to be supportive of this intervention.

Response three to the above scenario

The HR Director walks to the CEO's office and calmly explains that while she is excited about succession management as a critical business practice, before she puts anything in place a required level of maturity is required to introduce succession management. She asks for time to carefully research the most appropriate approach for the organisation and explains that the approach needs to be fit for purpose. She also highlights the risks and unintended consequences of doing succession management in an impulsive way, and explains the difference between succession planning and succession management.

Response four to the above scenario

The HR Director calls her team and debriefs them on the CE's expectations. She acknowledges that a commitment has been made and that there is a deliverable to be provided. She is not flustered as she has been lobbying for succession management with the executives for a few months. She has been analysing the HR metrics and has identified possible risks from the trend in data, so the CE's email is not a surprise. She has been proactively preparing for this outcome by already incorporating processes in the HR strategy. She has been focusing on improving the culture and been driving career management in the organisation. She has understood that succession management is a process and not an event.

Response five to the above scenario

The HR Director is surprised that the email she drafted a few months ago has finally been advocated by the Chief Executive. She prints out her change management process that she designed specifically for succession management and starts to implement the necessary steps, such as including the succession management business case for sign-off at the next executive meeting. She starts scheduling key meetings with each executive so that she can lobby for support before the executive meeting. The business case is comprehensive and addresses key issues as well as different scenarios.

Read the five scenarios and reflect which scenario is an accurate description of the dynamics within your organisation. Reflect on the five scenarios and identify which of the scenarios describes the response of HR most accurately. What are some of the inherent lessons in each scenario?

Scenario one

This is about reactively responding to requests without proper research or an in-depth understanding of the readiness of the organisation. This could be disastrous without considering the long term impact on the culture of the organisation. The inability to listen to concerns from the team does not demonstrate true leadership from the HR Director; risks may have been highlighted that could have been mitigated through the implementation plan.

Scenario two

This is often the approach that organisations follow, where the HR Director places the urgency for implementation above the fit and sustainability of the process. The "off-the-shelf" solution may be brilliant, however without understanding the culture and organisational climate, the solution is destined to fail.

Scenario three

This is a slight improvement to the first scenario as there is a conversation around clearing expectations and timelines, however the concern exists as to why research is only done after the fact. There should already have been a clear understanding of the organisational culture and a strategic long term plan with identified HR initiatives to be implemented. Succession management is in essence good HR planning and management.

Scenario four or Scenario five

Both responses in Scenarios 4 and 5 are excellent as they indicate that succession management has always been on the radar and that there was pro-activeness from the HR Director in lobbying and preparing for the change. There is also an indication of proper planning being done in the organisation.

Why was succession management placed on the table?

Let's explore what some of the real reasons for succession in an organisation are.

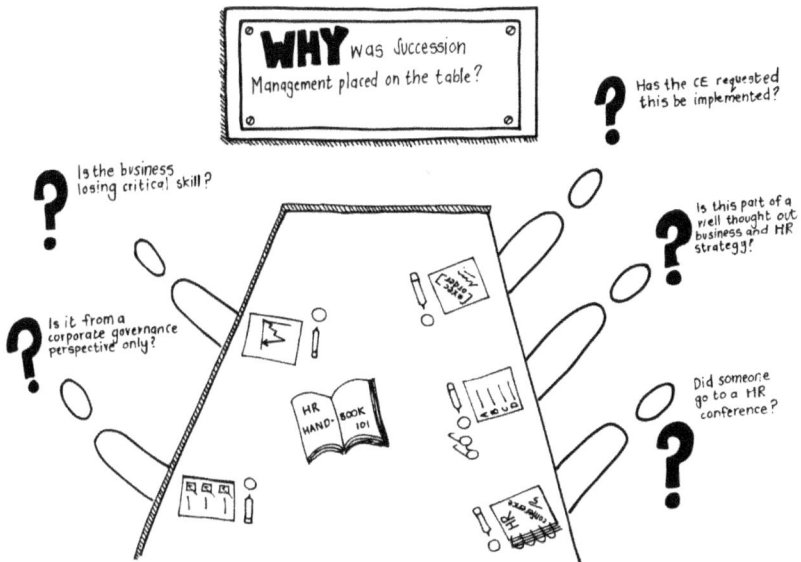

Is the business losing critical skills?

The first rule of sailing is to keep the ship afloat. Succession is like doing reactive maintenance on a ship that has sprung a leak, where there is a quick plug in.

If the ship already has lots of holes, using succession is not the smartest solution to plugging the holes. What is the point if the ship will continue to spring holes? You need to identify proactively what the best solution is from a preventative maintenance perspective.

You need to identify the cause of high turnover. What or who is making the ship leak? Succession is about sourcing internal talent from the organisation's talent pool; if your organisation has already lost employees to competitors, the talent pool is diluted and you need to strengthen it; it's like fishing in a pond where the fish have migrated and the fish you get is what is left behind. Implementing succession management as the only response will not ensure you get the strongest talent as you will be placing successors from a diminished pool. You need to first strengthen the pool through various graduate, designate and leadership programmes.

Is succession management part of corporate governance only?

The Board requires that succession management be implemented in the organisation to address business continuity risk. They are requesting to see a succession plan for all the executive roles. The danger with this is that succession management may be implemented for the sole purpose of compliance to the Board; it is the **letter of the law** and not the **spirit of the law** that is embraced.

Having an identified list of successors does not necessarily imply a commitment to transition successors to critical vacancies or an execution strategy to make this a reality. Usually the Board trusts leadership's commitment to develop identified successors and does not interrogate the process further.

Has the CE requested succession management be implemented?

Has succession management been identified as a critical HR practice by the executives as part of a broader talent management strategy? This approach presupposes that the difficult work has already been done to create a conducive environment to embed succession management. This approach is often the most appropriate, as proper planning is done to implement succession rather than a knee jerk reaction. Executive sponsorship is key in ensuring ultimate success.

Is this part of a well thought out business and HR strategy?

Is succession a natural progression of HR strategic projects rolled out in the organisation? This approach is the most likely to succeed since there is business sponsorship and probably sufficient resources allocated to the achievement of the succession process. Succession is viewed in relation to other HR practices and cultural readiness is determined before it is implemented.

Did someone go for an HR conference?

This may seem tongue in cheek, but most often someone attends an HR conference, sees succession management amongst other HR practices, and realises that they need to introduce it in their organisation. They may have good intentions, however is it the appropriate intervention at that point in time in their organisation? The decision to be made is whether succession management should be gradually rolled out through a phased approach or be implemented in its most sophisticated form.

As you will realise later in the book, there are a host of critical factors to consider when implementing succession management; having a succession process is only the tip of the iceberg.

Common succession management myths

There is only one correct succession management approach - False

Succession practice is about relevance and fit; there is no perfect approach that will be the panacea to all your talent challenges. The most appropriate solution is the one that makes sense to your organisation.

tips/ideas

Before jumping head first into succession management urgency, understand your environment, understand the nature of the request, and know the trigger for the request. This knowledge helps you to adequately prepare a business case for succession in your organisation, which enables you to understand risks and proactively identify mitigating actions.

Succession management is about replacing people – False

David Ulrich's view is that succession management doesn't start with people, but with the requirements of the position.[4] Since succession management is focused on addressing business continuity risk, the first step is always determining the business requirements and the responsibilities of a critical role before selecting successors.

Any organisation can implement succession management if there is an identified process to follow - False

There are certain prerequisites that need to be in place before implementing an organisational succession management process. There has to be a business case which addresses some key issues. There needs to be a proper understanding of why the organisation is implementing succession management. What is the scope of this process, i.e. which positions will be targeted for succession? Are these jobs properly defined in terms of outputs and competencies? What will this information be used for in the organisation? Will it be linked to any preferential incentives? How will it be linked to existing recruitment practices?

Succession is about having an heir apparent – False

An heir apparent is a person who is first in the line of succession and cannot be displaced from their inheritance. Succession is a dynamic process and may need continuous review as the business strategy changes. There should thus be no heir apparent as different skills may be more critical at various times in a business' evolution.

Succession management is an easy and speedy process to implement in the organisation - False

"One of the things we often miss in succession planning is that it should be gradual and thoughtful, with lots of sharing of information and knowledge and perspective, so that it's almost a non-event when it happens."[5] There are so many variables to consider when implementing a succession process; it may appear simple at first, but can potentially introduce additional complexities in the organisation once implementation occurs.

Succession management is about having identified successors for critical positions when they become vacant - False

Succession management is about effective business planning. It requires you to proactively develop people against a set of required competencies and experiences, rather than simply naming them as replacements. Succession is more than identification - it includes development and a transition into a new role. Once critical vacancies arise, successors are already in place with required levels of skill.

Succession management is decided by the Line Manager - False

The Line Manager does play a critical role by providing input into the suitability of an employee as a successor, however it is a misconception that the Line Manager has the final word on the issue. Succession management is decided through a process by a panel of people and often signed off by a talent committee. This is done in order to remove any form of favouritism and bias that may occur in the process.

Succession management is targeted at all roles in the organisation - False

Succession is about critical roles in the organisation, and whilst many feature in the senior roles, there are specialist jobs that by the nature of their contribution to the success of the business require a succession focus as well. You would never need a succession plan for the tea lady as there is often a plethora of possible candidates with the basic skills who can apply for the role.

Succession management is a passive process that is imposed on employees - False

Succession management is an active approach as certain steps are required to be followed which the employee participates in. The employee communicates their career interests, chooses to participate in assessments, and actively participates in their own development. The onus is on the employee to ensure that if chosen as a successor, they meet their developmental goals.

- Identify the trigger for succession and address the reasons for implementation. This always determines the approach you should adopt and can influence the success and sustainability of succession. The triggers are as follows:

  □ Loss of critical skill.

  □ Corporate governance.

  □ Executive request.

  □ HR strategic initiative.

  □ Recognition that it is a value adding practice.

- The hypothetical reflection depicts the typical business scenarios in South Africa of the usual reasons for why succession is introduced to the organisation.

- There are various myths about succession that an inexperienced HR practitioner may believe in. By debunking the myths, there is an accurate reflection of the true nature of succession.

Chapter 3

Building a business case for succession

....

> *When volatility, uncertainty, complexity and ambiguity is the current mode,*
>
> *How do you influence the executives to follow the winding succession road?*
>
> *Provide irrefutable proof of those businesses that have gone before,*
>
> *Their successes, their failures, the myths and the lessons they have endured.*

To build a compelling case for succession management, rather than using only best practice research to make your point, it is often more impactful to hold a mirror to the executives with statistics from your own organisation to reflect the anomalies, gaps and risks in people processes that directly impact the business. Be wary of painting a too dismal picture of doom and gloom, however; focus on the positive features as well, which you can build on with succession.

This means often connecting the dots of seemingly unrelated HR data to draw a picture of the present state of affairs in the organisation, such as low levels of engagement, high labour turnover, and a high record of absenteeism, which can indicate concerns in an organisation. Sometimes it also helps to draw comparisons with competitors if that data are readily available to make an even more compelling case. Also focus on the return on investment that proper succession practices bring to the organisation, and remember to link it to tangible business results.

Focus on the contribution to the business bottom line and the qualitative benefits to the organisation. For organisations that have never invested in succession management this may be a rude awakening, and to those that have basic replacement planning in place, how much work is required to get them on par may seem overwhelming. Your role is to paint an accurate picture of the organisation and provide a well thought out practical plan of how succession management will be implemented.

It is important not to overpromise to senior leadership, but to rather be realistic about the timeframes it will take to embed certain practices. The goal is not a tick box exercise, but a fit-for-purpose solution that best addresses your organisation's challenges. It takes time for succession to become mature - it cannot be transplanted into the organisation in its most sophisticated form. *That would be like giving a Ferrari to your unlicensed teenager and trusting that he would follow the rules of the road. It just isn't going to happen.* You need to emphasise that executive sponsorship is a non-negotiable in this process, and must be able to define the roles and responsibilities of the various stakeholders.

Your business case should focus on three parts: Where are you today?; Where do you want to be?; and How will you get there? Using the business case framework in Table 2 as a guide, develop a presentation and position it with your executives for sign-off. You need to include in your business case your subsequent recommendation and approach, given the context of the organisation and the readiness level. This means having a well thought out and executed plan of action, including timelines, roles and responsibilities, processes, education and embedding. This process differs in organisations and in some organisations approval may be an informal process. Remember the Chief Executive is usually the sponsor for this initiative, so it needs to be positioned and signed off at the correct level.

A business case framework for succession

Table 2: Business case framework for succession

	Core points to address in the business case	Why it is important
Where are you now?	What is the problem/ issue you are addressing?	Organisations face potential leadership vacancies, which can negatively impact business continuity; damage existing client relationships; affect critical business projects; and negatively impact team dynamics etc.

You need to build a case based on your organisation's information. Review your HR statistics in terms of age of workforce, labour turnover, length of time critical positions are vacant, and external versus internal recruitment statistics, and take actual examples of regretted losses. |
| Where do you want to be? | What are some key principles? | In your organisation, what are the principles that will govern the succession practice in your organisation? |
| | What are the lost opportunities and benefits? | Why should the organisation invest in this initiative? You can select from the benefits provided later in this chapter. |

	What are the roles and responsibilities?	This provides clear guidelines on who needs to complete which task so that nothing is omitted from the overall implementation plan.
	What executive decision is required?	Why are you doing the business case? Is it to share the status quo? Do you want to implement a strategy and need approval? What is your request from the executives?
How will you get there?	What is the high level succession process?	This provides an overview of the recommended succession process. Keep it at a milestone level rather than an activity level. You can craft the details once the business case is signed off.
	What is the high level implementation plan and timeframes?	This gives general project milestones and dates of implementation. This illustrates the link from the strategy to the implementation, and provides a realistic timeframe for implementing and embedding a new practice.
	What are the critical success factors?	This creates an awareness of what is additionally required for the implementation to be a success.
	What are the risks and mitigating actions?	This demonstrates that there has been proper deliberation over the anticipated hurdles in your organisation and you have considered strategies to address these.

What is the business rationale for succession management?

1. Organisations face potential leadership vacancies, which can negatively impact business continuity, damage existing client relationships, affect critical business projects, and negatively impact team dynamics and ultimately profitability and growth.

2. Succession management is a top priority for HR and Boards of Directors. According to the Corporate Executive Council, effective succession strategies drive revenue and profit outcomes by 12%.[6]

3. Succession management supports organisational stability and long term business sustainability. Without a succession process, organisations may not be able to ensure that programmes, products and services that are critical to operations are sustained after critical people have left. When critical employees leave the organisation, the vacancy creates an expected and accepted level of uncertainty with existing customers and a team of direct reports. When this vacancy is quickly filled by a successor, all traces of uncertainty are removed as there is an accountable person with the designated authority making the requisite decisions.

4. Succession enables the embedding of knowledge and experience as a tangible asset to be transferred. When critical employees leave organisations they take with them the organisational wisdom they have acquired throughout their careers, as well as their functional skills and knowledge. Succession management, if executed properly, will enable the easy transfer of this knowledge to identified successors. There should thus be a proper knowledge management process in organisations to ensure the seamless continuity of business processes.

5. There is a slight risk of unpredictability when external people are appointed at senior levels, but succession management provides an opportunity to predict the suitability of an internal candidate. Succession minimises the risk of recruiting external candidates into senior levels who may not be ready for the level of responsibility and are not properly acclimatised to the organisational culture. Recruiting external employees into senior levels also poses a bigger risk to the organisation, as they often make strategic business decisions that impact business processes. Without a proper understanding of the business culture, the pervasive business dynamics and their effects on business performance, an external appointee may exercise poor judgement and cost the business financially.

6. When successors come from within the organisation they are already acculturated and have established networks in place; they understand the organisation's vision, mission, values and strategic objectives. They are also familiar with the acronyms and terms that are specific to that organisation, which enables them to focus on their new role rather than spend time learning organisational specific information.

7. Building talent within sends a message to employees that they are important. Succession management research indicates that internal placement positively impacts employee engagement. Employees generally feel that there is some sort of progression or opportunity to grow in the organisation, and have a greater confidence that they will be given preference over the placement of external people.

8. Succession management promotes the organisation's reputation as an employer of choice that invests in its employees and provides development opportunities and support for promotion. Potential employees are attracted to organisations that appear to have embedded career management and succession management, which can add value to an organisation's talent acquisition strategy. This will assist the organisation to recruit external employees to critical roles where there are no identified successors. This will save unnecessary recruitment costs in

sourcing the appropriate people, as these people are more likely to want join the organisation.

9. Succession management provides for the development, replacement and strategic application of key people and processes over time to ensure that the organisation's long term business objectives are met. A developed talent pool that is prepared and available for any contingency allows the organisation to have greater control when deploying competent resources to strategic projects.

10. Succession management ensures that there is proper business continuity in the organisation, which will ensure a smooth transition of employees into critical roles. Successors are coached and supported once they move into vacant roles, which enables a more successful transition and communicates the organisation's continued support to the successor.

tips/ideas

It is critical to link succession to the strategic imperative of the organisation to ensure that there is leadership buy-in and sponsorship. It is necessary to also outline how this process can provide a competitive advantage to the business. There needs to be a positive pull factor of what can be achieved rather than only a push factor of all the outlined risks.

11. Finally, succession management ensures that proper career mapping for talented staff is done, thus enabling talent retention. Since the succession management process includes career management as an input into the process, this enables a proper career map for identified successors in the pool. This will serve as a retention factor for employees.

summary

- A business case is focused on three parts: Where are you now?; Where do you want to be?; and How will you get there?

- The business case must be presented to the executive for sign-off.

- The business case includes the scope of the initiative and informs the implementation plan.

- There are significant benefits to implementing succession management, including:

  - business continuity;

  - reduces the negative perception by clients;

  - drives revenue and profit outcomes;

  - supports organisational stability;

  - enables a culture of knowledge management;

  - deters the risk of having unknown people at senior levels;

  - decreases time to productivity for new hires;

  - communicates to employees that they are important;

  - builds the employer brand of the organisation;

  - enables the meeting of strategic objectives; and

  - promotes career mapping and competencies.

Chapter 4

Where is your organisation now?

....

It is important to have rules that every employee follows,

Rules that are understood by all, from the tea lady to the CEO.

These principles govern the scope of succession,

Defining specific responsibilities assigned to each role,

If not embedded will create a culture of blame, low trust and diminished leadership control.

Look objectively at your present organisation, not as an employee but as an external observer would view your organisation. Try to understand your present context. Look at your business lifecycle (is it a start-up or an established business) and business capability model[7] (are there recognised business capabilities embedded in the organisation), review the cultural maturity[8] and review the level of functional integration (e.g. HR works with IT on projects).

The old adage "Cut your coat according to your cloth" comes to mind. As a business trying to find a succession solution that is fit for purpose, you might choose the leading succession practice in the market as a benchmark, but there are a few things you need to consider before making that decision.

Just imagine you are an out-of-shape couch potato and you suddenly want to run a marathon. What are the reasons you want to run a marathon? Are they altruistic, like being in better physical shape for health reasons such as longevity or being a positive role model for your kids? Or is it because you are trying to keep up with the Jones'? Understanding the motivation differentiates the endurance and the level of discipline taken on sustaining the approach. You also need a sophisticated plan of action that includes an eating plan, a gradual exercise regime and a plan of action to gradually build up to running marathons. Your family may not support your goal and there is always chocolate cake in the fridge, or you may have a health condition that needs to be treated first. Similarly, if your organisation has numerous challenges, you need to first address the hygiene factors in the organisation. Be realistic when evaluating the 'shape' of the organisation before setting succession goals.

Organisational culture as an enabler

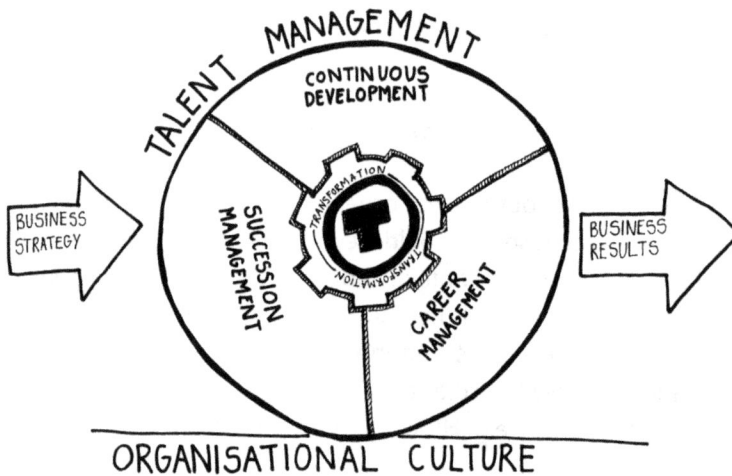

The organisation's business strategy is the trigger that initiates talent management.

Imagine talent management as a wheel that rolls towards business results; it propels the business strategy towards the achievement of the results. There are other HR spokes in the wheel, however for the purpose of this analogy I am going to focus on only three spokes, one of which is succession management and the other two being career management and continuous development. For the talent management wheel to be moving, all three spokes must be functional and working together. The width of the tire on the wheel is dependent on the structure of the wheel rim. Different organisations will have different wheel rims and thus tire widths. The ability of the wheel to roll smoothly depends on the smoothness of the surface. The organisational culture is the surface of the road. In some organisations the road surface is smooth, so culture enables the journey of the wheel towards results. When the surface of the road is unpaved, or worse yet has potholes, the wheel is more likely to be immobilised.

Peter Drucker is often credited with saying, "Culture eats strategy for breakfast". This statement can easily be applied to succession management. Favourable cultural factors are leadership credibility; a culture of trust; integrity; a culture of transparency; and a culture of courageous conversations, all of which provide a smooth surface for the wheel to roll easily towards its destination... business sustainability and business results.

Is the organisational culture conducive to succession management?

Introducing succession management to an organisation is like throwing a pebble into a still pond - it triggers ripples. The organisation is a system with various dynamics that are interdependent; any new practice that is introduced produces effects in other parts of the system. There may be unintended consequences that were never envisaged that now need to be managed. For example, an organisation with low levels of trust may be further negatively impacted with a poorly implemented succession process, which could lead to further levels of distrust and a toxic work environment. No matter how objective the evaluation criteria, the perception will be that the successor was unfairly selected. This leads to employee twitter posts like #Favoritismmustfall.

It is therefore important for you to do a culture readiness audit before committing to succession management. The culture in your organisation can either enable new practices or sabotage efforts to embed the new process. You may want to determine the readiness in your culture to adapt to new processes by using Annexure 1 – a readiness questionnaire. This questionnaire will assist you to understand the present state of readiness to implement succession management. If the score is relatively low then you need to first work on those elements to ensure that whatever new practice you introduce will be sustainable. The information can also assist in your business case to depict the present context.

Succession health check

The questions included in Table 3: Succession health check, can be included in your business case as part of illustrating the current organisational landscape. If you currently have succession management embedded in your organisation, how can you determine if it is working effectively? Your business case will be about taking cognisance of the current state of succession management and providing a remedial action plan to get it back on the right track.

The checklist in Table 3 will assist you to diagnose the amount of work still required for succession management. If you can answer 'yes' to most of the following questions, then you are already on your way to success.

Table 3: Succession management health indicator

	Indicator	Explanation	Yes (2)/ There is some work done (1)/ No (0)
1.	**Is there consensus amongst management on the key or critical roles in your organisation?**	Work has been done to identify the critical roles in the organisation, which will require the identification of successors. These critical roles are key to the business continuity of the organisation. The list of critical roles were identified, shared and signed off by the executives.	

	Indicator	Explanation	Yes (2)/ There is some work done (1)/ No (0)
2.	Do you know which are the scarce skills roles? Do you have programmes to replenish these scarce skills in your organisation?	Work has been done to identify skills that have unique requirements and are difficult to source in the market.	
3.	Is there a greater percentage of critical roles filled internally or through external recruitment?	If most leadership and critical vacancies are filled by external appointments, this indicates that succession is not working effectively.	
4.	Has there been a workforce analysis done in line with business strategy to identify future skills required?	This refers not to the current critical skills, but emerging skills that may be necessary with new product development or changing legislation etc.	
5.	Do you have responsive succession in place for these key roles, as well as those scarce skills profiles (business continuity, retirement, growing key skills)?	Relevant succession is focused on critical and scarce skills in your organisation. It is more than having an identification plan; it refers to the mobilisation of successors according to possible future scenarios. As certain positions may change, grow or be amalgamated, so succession is more than having a one-to-one ratio of current incumbents to successors; it should include potential candidates from a talent pool.	

	Indicator	Explanation	Yes (2)/ There is some work done (1)/ No (0)
6.	Does your succession process flow from a broader talent management process?	Succession management should start from a talent management framework to ensure that successors have met the criteria of consistent performance and future potential, as well as other criteria relevant for your organisation.	
7.	Are successors assessed and validated according to a predefined criteria?	Are successors assessed holistically according to their management and leadership potential, culture fit, learning agility and engagement levels, or are technical expertise and experience the only criteria?	
8.	Are there executive talent sessions to review successor progress against development goals?	Since business processes change so rapidly, a corresponding agile response to succession management is required. There has to be a continuous check on the pulse of the succession pool, using regular reviews that also ensure management commitment to successor development is monitored.	

	Indicator	Explanation	Yes (2)/ There is some work done (1)/ No (0)
9.	Is the organisation agile enough to review and adapt existing developmental goals to changing business strategies?	There must be a continuous assessment of whether new competencies are still required in the organisation, and a check on whether development plans are robust enough to incorporate changes.	
10.	Do you implement annual readiness assessments of successors?	There must be a robust process whereby successors are assessed against their achievement of agreed core competencies and signed off as competent with a portfolio of evidence.	
11.	Does your succession plan align with the employment equity plan and meeting of employment equity targets?	The succession plan should incorporate other key processes such as the workforce plan and the employment equity plan to ensure alignment.	
12.	Are you sure that your development budget is spent on identified successors to key roles to ensure readiness for the next key role?	There should be a special development budget for identified successors that includes focused development initiatives, rather than a broader development budget used for all employees.	

	Indicator	Explanation	Yes (2)/ There is some work done (1)/ No (0)
13.	Is there a transition plan in place for successors into critical vacancies?	There should be proper plans in place that enable easy transitions into vacant roles. This refers to introductions to stakeholder networks, clients, interdependent functional areas, and understanding cultural norms in the business unit.	
14.	Do you know what talent looks like in your organisation? Is there a common definition; philosophy; principles and an approach of talent and a shared mind-set amongst leaders of the demonstrated indicators in your organisational environment?	To ensure transparency in the succession process and to build trust amongst all stakeholders, there should be objective criteria that are consulted upon and agreed to before the process is applied to employees. This builds legitimacy in the process.	
15.	Do you know what leadership style is required in your environment?	There are different leadership styles, some of which are more relevant in certain industries than others. Are there defined leadership styles and competencies required in your organisation?	

	Indicator	Explanation	Yes (2)/ There is some work done (1)/ No (0)
16.	**Is there executive sponsorship of succession and is it viewed as a critical business process?**	Is the Chief Executive supporting and advocating the implementation of this process through holding executives accountable for non-delivery?	
17.	**Has there been a culture audit done and corresponding action plans created to prepare the environment for succession?**	This is not compulsory but provides great insight to resistance that might be encountered when succession is rolled out in the organisation.	

Succession maturity

Bersin & Associates and the Center for Creative Leadership published a report in April 2009, where they developed a model that differentiated succession maturity in organisations from succession in its most basic form to more advanced integrated succession practices.[9] They proposed the following scale:

Level 0: No succession process. This succession maturity is for organisations that do not have a real succession process in place and may limit succession to the Chief Executive role.

Level 1: Replacement planning. This succession maturity is for organisations that focus on identifying successors for senior roles with no focus on the development of these successors.

Level 2: Traditional succession planning. This succession maturity is for organisations that target senior critical roles, conduct talent reviews and implement development plans.

Level 3: Integrated succession management. This succession maturity is for organisations that have defined business strategies and critical roles that are aligned to those strategies. Succession extends to all critical roles and the succession process is integrated with other talent processes.

Level 4: Transparent mobility. These organisations fully understand the capabilities and potential of their workforce, with talent decisions being made effortlessly based on business requirements.

Transparent Talent Mobility
Dynamic process, highly transparent, pool-based, talent movement, professional and management roles

Integrated Succession Management
Business strategy alignment, talent management integration, enterprise perspective, owned by CEO

Traditional Succession Planning
Development plans, talent reviews, business-unit focus, targets key positions, HR-driven

Replacement Planning
List of senionr-level positions, list of high potentials, no development

No Succession Process
May include identification of successors of executive-level positions

Figure 4.1: Bersin & Associates' Succession Management Maturity Model® [10]

Where would you best place the maturity of succession in your organisation? Remember that the age of your organisation's process will not necessarily indicate its level of maturity. Succession management processes are iterative and are usually refined over time.

- This chapter discussed the importance of understanding the present context of your organisation.

- Culture plays a critical role in the positioning of succession in the organisation.

- A succession health check questionnaire can assess the effectiveness of succession in organisations practicing succession.

- The Bersin Maturity Model of Succession benchmarks different maturity levels.

Chapter 5

Where do you want to be?

> *What do you want to be known for, where do you want to be?*
>
> *Are you committed to implementing the succession process in totality?*
>
> *What are the key principles your organisation should embrace?*
>
> *What are the roles and responsibilities you should have in place?*
>
> *Are you starting off small and building your process as you go?*
>
> *Or are you determined to win brownie points with the CEO?*

You need to have an end picture of what you want succession to look like in your organisation; a compelling vision of what you want to move towards. This means you need to present more than a process to include how it can positively impact the organisation.

The World Health Organisation defines 'health' as a state of complete physical, mental and social well-being, and not merely the absence of disease or infirmity.[11] Similarly, creating a compelling business case for succession management is more than addressing all the risks of not doing it – it's also focusing on the positive benefits of implementing an effective integrated process. Taking the analogy further, what benefits would a healthy organisation derive in terms of business growth and sustainability? According to research there are numerous offshoots of a healthy organisation. What are the indicators of a healthy organisation? This means you need to research the specific benefits for your organisation. There are obviously generic benefits of having succession management effectively embedded in your organisation, but what are the explicit benefits that are industry- or organisation-specific that will contribute to long term positive changes in the organisation?

When you weigh the advantages and disadvantages of introducing large scale succession management in your organisation, there may be a view that the organisation is not ready for it or that the culture of the organisation will sabotage its effectiveness. The decision may be that keeping succession at the senior levels and not implementing a large scale change may best serve the organisation at this point in time. This decision, however, should only be made after the evaluation of the organisation's readiness and impact for change. If you plan to implement succession over a prolonged period of time, it is important to highlight the milestones for each year. The succession milestone table in Chapter 7 is an illustrative example of how you can stagger the process to build process maturity.

---

tips/ideas

- Building credibility for succession in an organisation takes time. To build and embed the process may take time. Sometimes gradual maturity and learning will happen as time passes.

- Sometimes the most critical aspects are executive support and understanding, and stakeholders' understanding of their roles and responsibilities during the roll-out of the process.

- The simpler the process, the easier the adoption and embedding of it in the organisation.

Once you have a good understanding of the present dynamics in the organisation, you need to map a path for succession. If you are not presently practicing succession management in your organisation, you need to have a realistic view of your succession goals. You need to also decide on the main principles that you want to adopt in your organisation.

The guiding principles you should consider for building succession

Here are some guiding principles, which are in no way an exhaustive list. Select the most pertinent principles for your organisation. You may need to develop additional principles not addressed in this book that cover organisation-specific requirements.

Principle 1: Sourcing through succession or recruitment

The most obvious question employees want answered is if they are a successor, can they automatically qualify for a vacancy or do they still have to apply formally for the role. This is a key principle decision that must be socialised with stakeholders, and after careful assessment of the implications of the various scenarios, an executive decision must be made. This must be done at the outset.

The following are basic options; other choices can be generated through a combination of options.

- **Option 1**: Advertise all vacancies.

- **Option 2**: Use succession plans as the only source for appointment into vacant positions.

- **Option 3**: The succession plan will be ringfenced for senior management to executive level roles as well as critical roles, where successors will be appointed from the succession plan. For the levels below all jobs will be advertised. The position will be advertised if there is no ready successor.

tips/ideas

Options	Advantages	Disadvantages
Option 1: Advertise all job vacancies	■ There is transparency in appointing employees through a selection process. ■ Allows all employees, including new employees who may have recently joined, an opportunity to apply for positions. ■ Eliminates perceived favouritism. ■ Prevents the feeling of entitlement with identified successors.	■ If successors are identified for the position, it may seem superfluous advertising a position. ■ Successors may not take the succession planning process seriously and this does not assist in the talent retention process. ■ The succession planning process may not be as robust as there is always a way out for managers from committing to succession plans.

tips/ideas

Options	Advantages	Disadvantages
Option 2: Use succession plans as the only source for making appointments	▪ Individuals identified for jobs will be properly developed according to the requirements of the job. ▪ Prevents a business continuity risk since successors can be appointed immediately. ▪ Successors already understand the business, the culture of the organisation and have established support networks. ▪ Serves as a retention measure.	▪ Will exclude high potential new candidates who could have recently joined the organisation. ▪ Roles in organisations are dynamic and individuals earmarked for jobs could no longer be relevant if business strategies change. ▪ May create a culture of entitlement with successors. ▪ Reduced competition and engagement of individuals not in the plan.

tips/ideas

Options	Advantages	Disadvantages
Option 3: Advertise jobs only if successors are not ready	▪ Successors are only appointed into identified positions if they are ready and competent, otherwise the job is advertised. This forces successors to continuously develop their skills.	▪ Successors may perceive the sign-off process to be unfair and not agree with the evaluation.

Principle 2: Confidentiality of information

A succession plan generates confidential data, both about individuals and the future structure of the group, and as such all data must be treated as highly confidential. It is recommended that only those directly involved in the collection and generation of data be party to the results of a review.

Principle 3: Communicating succession to successors

Employers share with employees that they are identified as talent, with the understanding that there is no implicit guarantee of appointment into a specific position without meeting developmental goals. Transparency gives the process legitimacy; it is like having an evacuation plan in the event of a fire, but no one has seen the plan and there has never been a drill testing its viability. A common category in succession management is emergency succession, which refers to the transition period from the time a vacancy arises to the

Principle 10: Validated through assessment

Identified successors will be assessed against objective criteria (leadership competencies). Whilst successors can potentially be nominated by a talent forum, they are validated only through the assessment process. Assessment will be comprehensive and assess different attributes including, but not limited to, technical expertise, personality, cognition, leadership competency, and emotional intelligence. Assessment should be holistic with a blended approach of psychometric and competency-based assessment to get appropriate information on an employee to make an informed decision.

Principle 11: Continuously measuring readiness

Successors are frequently reviewed through 360-degree evaluations and leadership assessments to assess their progress relative to their developmental goals. The 360-degree evaluation incorporates feedback from the successor's colleagues, direct reports and managers regarding whether the successor has achieved the required level of competence. This is important to measure readiness.

Principle 12: Adequate succession coverage

Successors will be sourced from a pool of talent, however there will be at least two successors identified for each critical role. When there are similar critical roles in the organisation then the number of successors per role may increase.

Roles and responsibilities

tips/ideas

Identify the most critical principles that are applicable for your organisation based on the industry, employee dynamics and HR processes.

As your succession process matures you can add additional principles. Remember principles must be fit for purpose.

Remember the principles serve as the foundation for your succession process and should support rather than hinder the implementation of the processes.

Based on your organisation you need to identify suitable roles and responsibilities for the succession management initiative. Table 4 provides a good foundation for the different roles and responsibilities, but in no way covers all possibilities.

Another way of presenting this information is through a RACI Matrix. This enables you to present each phase of the process and allocate corresponding responsibilities. Review Annexure 2 for an example of a RACI matrix.

tips/ideas

To ensure buy-in from all executives you need to lobby with the individual executives. Take them through your succession presentation and ask for their feedback. This enables you to divide and conquer and increases the probability of sign-off. They are not likely to ask difficult questions in the executive meeting when you have already done your homework and have consulted them. This also builds individual reationships and sponsorship. This lobbying is usually done by the HR executive in conjunction with the subject matter expert.

Table 4: Roles and Responsibilities

Executive	Senior Leadership	Line management	Talent/HR team	Employee
Supports the succession process. Provides the strategic future focus. Creates a culture of talent sharing across the business units. Monitors and ratifies succession plans for senior roles to ensure alignment to business strategy.	Approval and governance of the talent pool using the 9 box matrix, succession plans, and talent action plans. Ensures implementation of talent strategy and TM process. Models the leadership behaviour expected of others.	Identifies own successor. Manages talent through a process of engagement, gathering performance and potential feedback and evidence, performance management and coaching to ensure 'ready now' successors are available.	Facilitates the process. Sets clear goals and measures to implement the talent/ succession management strategy. Provides advice and support to line management. Ensures processes and templates are in place.	Reflects on career aspirations and goals. Ensures own career aspirations and development needs are communicated and plans agreed to that align individual and organisational needs.

Executive	Senior Leadership	Line management	Talent/HR team	Employee
Ensures that there is a developmental budget available for leadership development. Sanctions rotational assignments and other talent mobility initiatives. Commits their availability for talent review sessions.	Prepares and presents the succession plan and talent action plans (including sourcing, development and retention) for own department at the annual talent/ succession review session. Ensures the performance of other role players in the process. Continually monitors performance of the system. Manages the "politics" associated with the process.	Has focused career discussions with employees. Ensures talent action plans are implemented. Supports the process visibly. Evaluates staff objectively. Models the required leadership behaviour. Shares talent across the group. Acts as a coach transferring skills and experience. Provides feedback to successors on the talent session.	Builds capability to manage talent. Monitors and reports on talent activities and statistics. Develops competency profiles. Manages formal assessment processes. Documents outcomes of talent discussions. Measures and monitors succession readiness. Acts as an honest broker, frequently in the face of organisational political pressures.	Manages own career and development goals. Participates in experiential programmes. Achieves performance goals and remains committed to the organisation. Requests additional support when struggling with developmental goals. Is a positive role model of organisational values and ethics.

Summary

- The guiding principles for succession management were covered including:

  □ Sourcing through succession or recruitment.

  □ Confidentiality of information.

  □ Communicating succession to successors.

  □ Prerequisites for consideration for succession.

  □ Correct levels of sign-off.

  □ Awarding legitimacy to succession plans.

  □ Aligned to a broader talent management process.

  □ Sharing of organisational talent.

  □ Succession integrated into transformation agenda.

  □ Aligned to future business requirements.

  □ Validated through assessment.

  □ Measuring readiness.

  □ Adequate succession coverage.

- There are specific roles and responsibilities for different stakeholders: HR; Executives; Senior Leadership; Line Managers and Employees.

- You can use a RACI Matrix to visually depict the allocation of roles and responsibilities.

Chapter 6

How will you get there: A fit for purpose succession management process

When I implemented succession practices the executives were in awe,

Until the theory went into practice and they began to see the flaws.

My good intentions created chaos to all that it touched,

I forgot to assess the readiness and maturity so I implemented in a rush.

That was just the beginning of the drama that became worse,

I used an off-the-shelf solution not fit for purpose.

Line Managers went through the motions of the process like a tick box exercise,

The lack of commitment in the process brought it to a quick demise.

In the previous chapters the focus was on building your business case and getting the necessary sign-off. Once there is executive sign-off, the demanding work begins where you need to develop and implement a robust succession process.

Selecting an off-the-shelf succession process

If you have a zero base and need to start developing a succession process, where do you begin? Most people start by enthusiastically looking at best practice models developed in other organisations and think it is a simple process of finding the best and then transplanting it into an existing system. The challenge with this approach is that best practice for one organisation can unfortunately be a total misfit for another.

The internet is flooded with succession processes and models, and it may be tempting to look for fancy sophisticated models that can impress the executives. How do you decide which model or process is best for your organisation? I would like to offer a few criteria you can consider. Whilst I also include a simple process later on in this the book, you must peruse different models to be able to evaluate what is most fit-for-purpose in your organisational context. Table 5 below includes questions you can pose when comparing different succession management processes.

Table 5: Key considerations when choosing succession processes

1. Is the approach relevant to your organisation, for example does it include critical roles and not only executive succession?

2. Does the model and process easily integrate into existing HR processes?

3. Are there foundational HR practices that your organisation has embedded which will align with the new succession process, for example are career management conversations occurring?

4. Is the succession process simplistic and can it be easily replicated across functions in the organisation?

5. Are the concepts and processes easy to explain and understandable to others in the organisation?

6. Does the succession process include all the change and communication stages?

7. Does the succession process and model use straightforward language or complicated jargon?

8. Are there demarcated roles and responsibilities for all stakeholders?

9. Does the process allow you to gradually build business maturity through a phased roll out?

10. Can this succession process be easily cascaded to other levels in the organisation?

Designing and implementing a succession management process

Table 6: Succession management milestones

Year one: Prepare for succession	Year two: Implement the succession plan	Year three: Measure and correct	Year four: Reinforce and evolve succession practice
Understand the succession management practice need or request.	Create a change and communication plan to influence the mindset change.	Assess the nominated successors against suitable assessment criteria to identify development areas and confirm successor suitability.	Measure succession through talent metrics which have identified talent bench strength and succession coverage in critical roles.

Year one: Prepare for succession	Year two: Implement the succession plan	Year three: Measure and correct	Year four: Reinforce and evolve succession practice
Research the organisational culture and readiness for succession. Identify key risks and issues.	Develop training focused on adult learning principles that include simulations and role plays to develop managers.	Provide feedback to successors and develop and sign-off individual development plans.	Identify a suitable technology platform to enable the process in future.
Develop the business case based on organisation-specific variables such as business strategy, business specific critical roles, and people challenges.	Implement training by rolling it out to all relevant Line Managers.	Source suitable development interventions and development opportunities for successors.	Identify suitable retention incentives for successors.
Socialise and sign-off the business case with the executives.	Implement the process, manage and monitor succession process completion.	Monitor progress of development through feedback reports.	Engage successors through continuous discussions.
Design a succession management policy and process.	Hold succession reviews with business and complete succession templates.	Schedule talk about talent sessions with managers to discuss succession progress and review the validity of existing successors.	Ensure succession development and readiness is built in Line Manager key performance indicators.

Year one: Prepare for succession	Year two: Implement the succession plan	Year three: Measure and correct	Year four: Reinforce and evolve succession practice
Sign-off the succession process, succession policy, critical roles and implementation plan.	Collate data and sign-off the nomination list of identified successors.	Get feedback on succession process and refine the process, templates and timelines.	Identify a mentor other than the manager to help the successor navigate through broader organisational challenges.

Understand the succession management practice need or request

This was discussed extensively in Chapter 2 and refers to understanding how the need determines the succession approach you will take.

Research the organisational culture and readiness for succession

You can use the culture readiness questionnaire in Annexure 1 to determine readiness to implement succession.

Imagine for a moment that implementing succession is like climbing a ladder. You have to climb to the top of the ladder by starting at the bottom and only when you know the ladder is on a stable surface will you be comfortable climbing. The rungs of the ladder refer to the succession maturity in the organisation.

How many people are allowed on the ladder? A minimum number otherwise it creates a risk. Similarly, in an organisation you need to ensure that whilst you are busy climbing, there aren't too many other people climbing behind you and implementing new practices before you had a chance to implement succession. The risk is that you can lose your balance and fall off.

The correct way of climbing a ladder is the three point approach; at any point there are three points in contact with the ladder - two hands and one foot. The other foot is positioned to already move onto a higher rung. This means that when you introduce new practices in an organisation, you always embed what you have done and ensure there is continuity before moving on.

> *It is usually the executive who decides against which wall the ladder should be positioned. The context is very important. Where is the ladder? Is it in a stable environment with a solid floor or is it on a mountain ledge with gale force winds? The environment is important in understanding the risks involved in climbing the ladder. If you are working in a stable environment with relatively few changes, climbing the ladder is easy. If you are in a volatile environment and an industry that keeps reinventing itself, climbing the ladder is going to be more challenging. Does the ladder keep moving against different walls as business strategies change?*
>
> *How high do you need to climb? In some organisations with a mature culture of HR management, you get a boost up the ladder. There is less risk since the leadership is standing at the base of the ladder providing encouragement and stability. How confident are you that your leadership will support your climb up the ladder?*
>
> *How resilient do you need to be to climb the ladder? What are the skills and competencies you need to adapt to any sudden business strategy changes? Are you able to build in scenarios where the business radically changes and the people requirements mean going back to the drawing board?*

Develop the business case

Develop the business case based on organisation-specific variables such as business strategy, business-specific critical roles and people challenges. A business case framework is included in Chapter 3 and covers the relevant information to be considered such as business maturity and business lifecycle.

Talent pools are the vehicles for translating the business strategy into the HR strategy in order to deliver on the business plan. Strategically appropriate talent pools are shaped by asking the question, "Are the organisation's investments aimed at the talent areas that are most critical to the strategic success of the business?"

Elements that can be considered when identifying critical roles in your organisation may be around the contribution of the roles to the bigger business strategy; the roles that drive revenue and business growth; the impact on the organisation if a role no longer existed; and the degree to which business processes would be interrupted should there be a vacancy in a role. Once the talent pool has been defined to meet organisational success, the talent strategy to attract, retain, develop and deploy people to fill that talent pool will be aligned with the corporate strategy. These talent pools facilitate the movement from role-based succession reviews to business needs-based succession reviews.

Socialise and sign-off the business case

The succession business case provides intent to the Chief Executive; it demonstrates that succession was researched, evaluated in-depth, and organisation-specific recommendations were tabled. Implementing succession is easier when you lobby with your CEO for support; his sponsorship paves the way for effective implementation.

Design a succession management policy and process

A succession policy is necessary in a succession management practice as it provides legitimacy to the selection of successors as well as in the appointment of these successors to critical roles. The succession policy is aligned to the recruitment policy and they often work in tandem. The succession policy must have the necessary principles and allude to the governance and objectivity of the process. You can select from these basic principles in Chapter 4.

Sign-off the succession process, succession policy, critical roles and implementation plan

As previously discussed, executive buy-in and sign-off is non-negotiable. This is a mandate that paves the way for succession to be rolled out without unnecessary resistance. The sign-off of critical roles assists the executive to take ownership when deciding the scope of succession in the organisation.

Create a change and communication plan

Create a change and communication plan to influence the mindset change. A change approach ensures that communication and training occur at the right time in the right context, makes sure employees have the answers they need regarding succession in the organisation, increases the speed of adoption of the new succession process, reduces the number of barriers or obstacles experienced (succession is a sensitive process and there are often high levels of resistance from different role players), and encourages sustained results for the initiative and embeds it into the organisation. Refer to Annexure 3 for an example of a change and communication plan. If you want to determine a successful outcome then you need to limit the variables by scripting everything. You can script emails from executives, to career conversation guides to the structure of feedback.

Develop training material

Training materials can be developed with succession templates and concepts. The purpose of designing succession training is to create a common succession language in the organisation for managers to understand the process and templates. You can choose to develop training material from some of the concepts discussed in this book or those you have reviewed in other literature; the key lesson is that the training material should be comprehensive enough to incorporate all aspects of succession and provide a realistic view of how the process may be implemented. Use adult learning principles and develop a more interactive training approach with suitable role plays and simulations. There should be an exercise on choosing suitable successors based on fictitious case studies, while career conversation simulations provide a safe environment for managers to practice their skills. You need to provide difficult scenarios in the training module to work through, as if they competently perform in these scenarios, they will be adequately prepared for reality. Refer to Annexure 4 for a sample of training outcomes you could include.

Implement training

You can train managers directly if you have a small organisation, or use a train the trainer approach in large organisations. By training managers on the succession process, you create a common mindset around talent and help them identify and develop successors easily. Training is more than sharing the methodology, definitions and templates - it should include simulations and practice exercises of career conversations to prepare managers. A simulated succession review session also provides confidence and comfort for managers, so that they support the process in its entirety. Face-to-face training is essential as often managers learn from each other's unique circumstances and concerns. You can also assess at this early stage which managers will resist the succession process and you can address their concerns timeously.

Implement the process, manage and monitor succession process completion

At the outset, strategically position the initiative by sending out a memorandum from the Chief Executive. This introduction sets the context for you to implement the succession initiative without organisational resistance. Annexure 5 is an example of an email that can be sent that sets the context for succession, but if your organisation is more formal, this may need to be rewritten. To reinforce this message, the Senior Manager should send the communication to Line Managers with further instructions (Annexure 6). When the Line Manager is sent the necessary templates from his manager (Annexure 7: Career questionnaire, Annexure 8: High-potential forms and Annexure 9: Talent profile), there is more likely to be a positive response rather than resistance. In Annexure 7 there are sample career questions you can include; these are basic questions which you can build on to elicit more information. Annexure 8 is the high-potential form which includes some popular competencies that organisations include in their definition of high-potential. You need to customise this to your organisation.

Monitoring the completion of the necessary templates is the most tiring phase in the process as it requires Line Managers to have career conversations with their direct reports, and complete high-potential forms and talent profiles in the required timeframes. You will be continuously reminding both Line Managers and employees to follow the process. It is important that there is an established deadline that is communicated to all Line Managers. Be available to answer questions or to clarify the approach taken. From my experience you need to build in at least two extra weeks in your deadline, because people will submit late. Sometimes when they do meet the required timeframe, you will find that the information is still incomplete.

There should be a career discussion as part of the normal performance discussion. Employees should indicate interest in possible roles in the organisation. This will be used to properly match individuals to successor roles based on their interests and competence.

Hold succession reviews across the business

A succession review is a meeting where senior leaders discuss talent information and subsequently succession. The succession or talent review is usually an opportunity to calibrate with other managers the high-potential standard and to compare high-potential talent across the business. It also creates a safe environment for managers to discuss their people. This requires Line Managers to have a sufficient depth of understanding of their employees to be able to discuss them confidently. It also creates an opportunity for dialogue with other managers around perceptions and reality. It is critical that the person presently occupying the role should give input on the suitability of the candidate as she understands the job complexity, while managers get an opportunity to understand the talent availability in other parts of the business.

tips/ideas

HR's role in the facilitation of succession sessions

- Agree to meeting rules and be the custodian of these rules in the session.

- Facilitate the succession management process.

- Nominate a scribe to capture conversations.

- Challenge the Line Managers to consider the person holistically.

- Ask managers to motivate why they feel their nominee has the potential to be a successor. Ask them to refer to the potential criteria form to motivate their view.

- Capture comments verbatim about each nominee and write this information down. It may be helpful to ask one of the managers to be your scribe so the discussion is not lost whilst you are facilitating.

- Be the mirror and reflect the business reality.

- Challenge the cognitive biases by asking for objective evidence of behaviour.

- Ensure that each Line Manager is given a fair distribution of talk time. Do not let anyone dominate the discussion.

- Facilitate completion and sign-off for the succession template.

Collate data and sign-off the validation of identified successors

Post the succession session, all the necessary documentation must be completed. This includes the motivation for certain employees who are identified as successors as well their talent profile, and a consolidation of all the input received from other managers in the session. Circulate the final succession template (Annexure 10) to managers for sign-off before proceeding to the next step. This allows sufficient time to deal with managers who suddenly develop amnesia on why certain employees were selected over others. Annexure 10 is a generic succession template and can be customised according to your business requirements. To ensure integrity in the process, make sure all information is documented and circulated. You can populate the succession template into a more visual representation (Annexure 11) of the succession status in the department with the organogram for the department. This provides a more impactful view and tells a robust story about which roles indicate a high vacancy risk.

Assess the nominated successors

Assess the nominated successors against suitable assessment batteries to identify development areas. There are a range of valid and reliable assessment batteries in the market. Once again, the choice of assessment should fit into your organisation's unique circumstances and culture. It is important that assessment as a practice and discipline is supported by the executives and that there is a high level of understanding and credibility. Also remember to set a suitable benchmark for assessment that considers the industry's and the organisation's performance. Organisations often make the assumption that each person can learn to be competent in almost anything, however it is important to acknowledge that certain competencies may be very difficult for a successor to develop later, so be realistic about choosing successors and their learning agility to cope at the next level of complexity; assessments must be holistic and view successors through different lenses.

At this stage there may be many nominated successors who fall off during this process since their assessment results do not support the initial views of the committee.

Feedback to successors

Provide feedback and develop and sign-off individual development plans. As discussed, if successors are not informed that they are on a succession plan, they will not be able to develop the necessary expertise and readiness for identified roles. The process of feedback must be done in a manner that does not create unnecessary expectations. Once employees receive their assessment feedback, they should incorporate this into their development actions within specific timeframes. It is necessary that all successors have signed-off development plans. It is also critical that there is a focused development budget for these development interventions. Do not create unrealistic development expectations with successors; sometimes organisations string employees along and never plan to appoint an individual into a critical role, as they want to retain the employee for their present contribution and not their future contribution.

Source suitable development interventions

Source suitable development interventions and development opportunities for successors, as it is important to align expectations with reality. This means that there should not be unrealistic development expectations about the timeframe for successors to become ready for the identified roles. Line Managers or the current job incumbents need to meet the successors where their development gaps are presently. The common mistake is that managers expect that the same recipe that was used for them to acquire their experience, knowledge and skills will be the appropriate recipe for the successors to follow. The error in this logic is that the world has shifted and there are newer learning processes and techniques. Learning has also evolved from the traditional classroom based model to a more interactive e-learning methodology. It is therefore necessary to understand the learning style of the successor and provide the necessary wisdom in that learning context.

There is an overwhelming abundance of information in the wisdom age, therefore the challenge is not the access to information, but the judgement of what information is relevant to make the correct decision.

In addition there has been a shift to the 70: 20: 10 learning and development model, which is broken down as follows:

- The 70% - Experiential/Experience - learning and developing through day-to-day tasks, challenges and practices.

- The 20% - Social/Exposure - learning and developing with and through others using coaching, exploiting personal networks, and other collaborative and co-operative actions.

- The 10% - Formal/Education - learning and developing through structured classroom–based learning courses and programmes.

If you really want to develop and stretch your leaders then you need to focus on more experiential development. There are many books and websites available that provide further insight into sustainable and dynamic leadership development that can navigate the volatile and uncertain business environment. The most common approach presently is through stretch experiences, which are planned and focused development initiatives that widen the successor's worldview.

Monitor progress of development

Monitor the development through feedback reports; if it is not tracked and monitored, a succession plan is just a list of names with no real business value. It is therefore key that development plans are executed and that there is a level of accountability from the potential successor as well as the Line Manager. This will ensure a strong leadership bench strength and credibility in the process going forward.

Schedule 'talk about talent' sessions

Schedule 'talk about talent' sessions to discuss succession progress and to review the validity of existing successors. The sessions usually occur three to four months after the succession review. The intention is to track developmental progress and for Line Managers to provide additional insights into the different successors. The session is usually a short, focused session where each successor and their progress is reviewed.

Get feedback on the succession process

Get feedback on the succession process and refine the process, templates and timelines. Once the first cycle of succession has taken place it is necessary to get feedback on the process. Determine the feedback through short surveys of Line Managers. You can use the feedback survey in Annexure 13. Use this feedback to improve the process and templates going forward. If there are concepts that Line Managers are still struggling with, organise a refresher training event.

Measure succession through talent metrics

Talent metrics are used to measure the identified bench strength and the succession coverage in critical roles. You need to prove to executives that there are defined measures for succession and that there is a return on investment. This means providing regular metrics at the executive meetings to keep momentum and reaffirm support of the process. This is discussed in Chapter 8 in more detail.

Identify a suitable technology platform

Beware of placing the cart in front of the horse; identify a suitable technology platform to enable the process in the future. Many organisations commit the sin of buying an HR technological platform and then try to design the succession process around the available technology. The problem with this is that managers associate succession with filling in data and fail to see the importance of the conversations and engagement - the holistic process. Technology should enable the succession process rather than dictate it.

Automation definitely helps speed up the process, however it does not replace the change management and education that is required in the business. Once your succession is embedded with the correct discipline then investigate which technology will streamline the process.

Identify suitable retention incentives for successors

All employees are unique and you cannot make assumptions that what motivates one individual will motivate another. Everyone assumes that money is the key driver for retention, but research has found differently. Some people may want money, however others may be motivated by access to senior leadership or exclusive committees, positional power or status. The trick is to identify an employee's top values and design incentives for the individual, rather than following a cookie cutter approach which assumes all talent are driven by the same desires. Respecting and acknowledging this diversity among talent can be the difference between success and failure. Even though people may be in a talent pool, you need to understand their distinctive characteristics, and you will be rewarded by engaged employees who feel appreciated. There is thin line between making people feel appreciated and making them think they are unique and special however - the latter breeds a sense of entitlement.

People challenges to succession management

There are often people challenges encountered in succession management, as perspectives about individuals are often different. What compounds this are organisational politics that amplify differences in opinions and lead to subtle power games.

Understanding and managing the emotions attached to succession management

Succession management is an emotive process and it is important that you are sensitive to the behavioural dynamics. The following scenario gives you an opportunity to experience first-hand some of the emotions linked to succession.

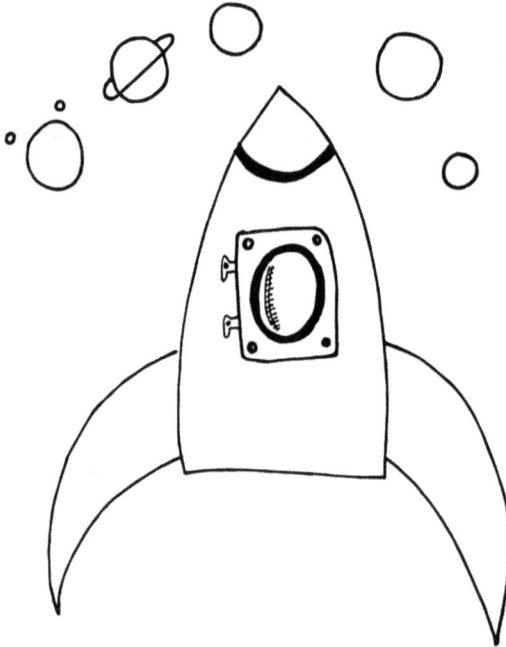

Hypothetical scenario

Imagine that you were offered a once-in-a-lifetime opportunity to start life on a new planet. You are a renowned world expert on succession. The world is dependent on your expertise for environmental sustainability. The condition is that you cannot return to Earth again. Your departure is in two years. There will be access to communication and you will be able to Skype your family. You are really excited about this opportunity but you are devastated about leaving your husband and two teenage boys behind. You have a wonderful husband and a great family. Your husband was your childhood sweetheart and he has grown up with you and is always supportive of your dreams and career aspirations. After a few days of reflection you have the courageous conversation with him. He is devastated with the news but comes around after a week and becomes selfless and supportive of this opportunity. His one condition to you is to find him a successor who will take your place. He says you need to do the selection since you best understand the requirements of the position having known him for 30 years and having been married to him for 15 years. He also says that you need to break the news to your mother-in-law and suggests she must assist you in the search. He further suggests that you look within your close network of friends since there are a few single women available. He requests that it would help if the successor is attractive. Then he says let the potential successors join you on your family holiday in Mauritius so he can assess family cultural fit and suitability.

How do you approach this task? What emotions are you experiencing? What are you really thinking now?

Having shared the scenario with various people, there is an overwhelmingly similar response from individuals who cannot fathom having someone take their unique place; most people are unable to separate emotion from the actual decision. Since it personally involves you, you are able to imagine the conflicting emotions that line leaders often experience when selecting a successor.

Employees tend to build their identity around their jobs and some managers become quite territorial when asked to consider successors. Some managers feel their job security is threatened by choosing a successor, and do not want to identify people who can potentially surpass their legacy. When they do choose successors, it is people who are always in the 1 to 2 years readiness category. These employees never move out of this category and become ready for these roles, so they eventually get frustrated and leave the organisation. The Line Manager is relieved as he has once more secured his job. This situation can be averted by leadership who notice these anomalies, challenge these perceptions, and become actively involved in successor selection.

The handover of expertise

The example below further illustrates this phenomena of Line Managers' relationships with successors.

Once upon a time in the animal kingdom, the Lion was getting old and was ready to retire, so he looked at his five cubs who were three years of age and ready to leave the pride. It was time for the Lion to choose his successor. He had developed his sons in the key leadership skills of hunting, combat and general survival. The Lion knew that given the changing environment in the animal kingdom, these skills were not sufficient for adapting to the new world. Climate change meant more drought, less food and fewer animals, and the forest was plagued by more storms. Now that man had started to hunt, no animal was safe. This volatile and uncertain world required a new breed of leadership. The Lion understood that there is strength in diversity, so he called his wise counsellors together who suggested that the cubs experience some form of stretch assignment to take them out of their comfort zone. The Lion carefully selected mentors from the different animal classes based on the development gaps of each of his cubs. Each mentor could teach a lion cub a different skill and prepare them to deal with adversity. The five mentors were the Wolf, the Fox, the Lark Bunting Bird, the Cuckoo and the Hyena. Three months of the internship passed and the Lion called his cubs together to determine each one's readiness to succeed to the throne.

The Fox

The lion cub who lived with the Fox had the least to say. He told his father how every time he followed the Fox to learn new skills, the fox deliberately misled him. The fox evaded the lion cub by running up or down streams, running along the tops of fences and using other tactics to throw off the lion cub. The lion cub was tired and hungry as the Fox did not share his food, but instead had stored his food in hideouts to be consumed at a later time. The lion cub was very disillusioned by his experience with the Fox. The Lion King was furious and exiled the Fox from the kingdom until he could learn his lesson to share his knowledge and skills openly.

Lesson 1

You may have managers who have reached their career ceiling and plan to protect their job, or a few managers close to retirement who are reluctant to jeopardise their legacy by finding more competent successors. They are the Hoarders and they have built their identity with their jobs and want to be remembered as the best there ever was. They appear to be sharing their wisdom but they often delegate unimportant tasks to successors to keep them busy. This is purely an egocentric response. You need to watch their behaviour carefully as they will sabotage successors or worse yet, fail to identify suitable successors so that their role remains secure. They just cannot share the limelight; they will destroy the credibility of their successors and deliberately frustrate them so that they will resign.

The Lark Bunting Bird

The Lion called the cub who was mentored by the Lark Bunting Bird who had a different experience from his brother. The Lion had deliberately chosen a bird over an animal as he wanted his son to learn about seeing the world from a different perspective. The Lion understood that to respond with agility it was important to also be able to envisage the long term risk. The lion cub told his father that he learned to look at the same information from different perspectives. Another lesson the lion cub received was adaptability. He told his father that the Lark Bunting chose a mate each year with different characteristics that were based on the feedback of the environment. The Lion was impressed with the great life lessons that the bird had imparted.

lark

Lesson 2

In a dynamic work context there has to be a continuous review of information for relevance; learning often happens in real time and the successor needs to be agile to deal with the changing environment. The manager is a Lark Bunting Bird that is able to adapt his managing style from one situation to another. Rather than transferring stagnant information, the manager transfers the ability to deal with changing contexts and demands and breeds resilience. In the new VUCA world, information quickly becomes obsolete so the ability to identify relevant solutions, undertake analyses and exercise judgement is more valuable.

The Cuckoo Bird

The lion cub who was paired with the Cuckoo then gave his feedback. Given the last impressive report, the Lion waited patiently for a similar response. The lion cub puffed his chest as he recalled his time with the Cuckoo, and told his father that he learned that he didn't really have to do anything on his own. The cub explained how the clever Cuckoo bird tricks other birds into raising her own youngster, freeing her up to enjoy life as a single bird. She does this by laying her eggs in the nest of another bird. This way she no longer needs to build her own nest. "So father, you see, I don't have to do any hard work, I can just let others do the work and I can take the credit." The King was furious since the core values he had instilled in his son about a sense of duty and responsibility were washed away by a poor role model.

cuckoo

Lesson 3

The Cruisers are terrible role models who are more focused on the delivery of their own objectives and do not make time to transfer knowledge or skills to others. They cruise in the last few years pre-retirement, rarely caring about the readiness of their successor. You need to identify these characteristics early on to handle these managers appropriately.

The Wolf

The lion cub who studied under the Wolf was eager to share his feedback. He said that he was inspired by the wolves as they worked together in a collaborative way; they hunted together and then shared their food with the weaker, younger wolf cubs. The lion cub said he had learned the competency of co-operation and team work, and went on to talk about the easy way in which information was shared with him. The Lion was very impressed and called the Wolf and nominated him as the Most Empowering Leader in the forest.

Lesson 4

It is easier to identify successors for managers who are young and talented and have the potential and capability to move into other positions, as they are Sharers who view jobs as stepping stones to a greater career goal. You may find mature managers who are Sharers, however they are very scarce. Sharers take succession in their stride and are often shocked by the notion that not all managers share information like they do. They understand that their promotability is highly dependent on the availability of competent people in their team. Sharers understand that they are dispensable and therefore do not tie their identity to their job roles. If they do, this identity is loosely linked, as they see their job as a temporary role that they are playing that they can leverage off for another role in the future. These Sharers continuously upskill themselves and keep their knowledge and skills relevant and up-to-date.

The Hyena

The Lion called the last cub who had done his internship with the Hyena. The lion cub said he was not impressed with the striped Hyena who was not at all sociable. The Hyena often appeared to be sharing hunting knowledge with the lion cub, however when it came to the actual hunt, the Hyena and the lion cub fought over the same territories as they hunted the same prey. When it came to the time to eat, the Hyena often ate all the food leaving nothing for the lion cub. The lion cub said that he never really felt he could trust the Hyena, which led to fierce competition between the two animals. The Lion was not impressed and asked the cub what one lesson he had learnt from the experience. The cub promptly responded that it was: "Never impart all your knowledge and keep some tricks for yourself." The Lion shook his head in deep sorrow as he realised that no meaningful knowledge was really shared.

Lesson 5

There are some managers who are supportive of the succession process and are the perfect role models for succession as they motivate, inspire and coach their successors. This usually continues until the moment when they realise that their successor is suitably equipped and with a little refinement is ready for their role. They have an invisible line drawn that if crossed, triggers an attitude change. They start off as Sharers and then their behaviour radically shifts to the other extreme, where they become unsupportive and subtly start to sabotage their successors through incorrect feedback in the succession reviews. These are the "Change of Heart" managers, who are the most difficult to spot. It is thus important to calibrate their successor's development progress and notice if there is suddenly contradictory feedback. A good illustration of this point is through the popular fairytale Snow White, where the wicked stepmother's relationship with Snow White is acceptable as long as the stepmother was the most beautiful person in the kingdom and Snow White never surpassed her beauty. The moment that Snow White became beautiful, the stepmother's feelings towards Snow White radically changed and she wanted her removed.

The Lion's lesson was to be careful of the individuals you select as role models for successors. Their behaviour is often replicated by the successors as ideal and acceptable behaviours that should be adopted. The Lion realised that out of the five lion cubs, only two had developed deep insight and should be included in the succession pool.

Realising that they were the two selected successors, the attitude of the cubs towards each other started to deteriorate where they started to compete on the silliest of things. If something went wrong they blamed each and took no accountability for their mistakes. The King was highly upset with the childish behaviour of his cubs and had a long discussion about the culture they were creating in the animal kingdom. The King also realised that he had extremely high expectations for his cubs when they were still very young, impressionable and likely to make many mistakes.

Lesson 6

You may find that successors play political games. If the organisational culture is not mature, succession can lead to unhealthy competition with people playing corporate politics to undermine other colleagues for a position. Succession games are damaging to the organisation, thus it is important to identify the presence of this behaviour and deal with it effectively. This can often indicate the level of emotional maturity of successors and may provide contradictory evidence of their eligibility and readiness. It is important to confront this behaviour with the individuals concerned.

Lesson 7

The greatest mistake organisations make is placing successors on a pedestal or the **golden throne**. This is a typical example of the halo effect, where an organisation will assume that a successor has all the necessary qualities and characteristics and can do little wrong. When they are guilty of some transgression, the disappointment is amplified tenfold; the higher the pedestal the greater the fall. Successors often fall out of favour quickly because organisations have unrealistic expectations and fail to communicate these. It is important to understand that successors are still employees who are susceptible to similar folly like other employees.

Recognising different forms of bias

The challenge is to identify talent as they are and not how Line Managers perceive them. Managers need to be aware of various cognitive biases they may experience in selecting successors. A **cognitive bias** is a systematic error in thinking that affects the decisions and judgments that people make.

Don't you just love how old stuff is renamed vintage and suddenly the value increases? Given the changing context, employees who were never deemed great by the organisation can be reevaluated against high-potential criteria and be assessed as fit-for-purpose. Viewing employees without the lens of unconscious bias can mean employees once deemed unsuitable may be re-examined more objectively.

An example of one such bias is **confirmation bias**. Once people have formed a view, they embrace information that confirms that view while ignoring, or rejecting, information that casts doubt on it. Confirmation bias suggests that people do not perceive circumstances objectively but pick out those bits of data that make them feel good because they confirm their prejudices.[12] It is very difficult to change a perception of a manager who has already labelled a potential successor as a non-effective contributor, or vice versa, seeing a non-effective contributor as a high-potential successor. It is incumbent on the succession facilitator to elicit sufficient evidence on the employee to overcome this bias. For example, an employee may be a great performer and a specialist, however this does not necessarily mean that they have great future leadership potential or that they can work in a role with greater complexity.

Jason was a brilliant financial analyst and he had received consistent praise for all his contributions, until he started to work with his new manager who developed a personal dislike to him. The new manager did not appreciate Jason's need to challenge the status quo and that Jason was seen as the unofficial leader of the department who was highly regarded by his peers. The new manager rated Jason as having little potential to succeed him and despite the overwhelming positive feedback would not change his mind. The senior manager who had received reports from Jason and admired his fortitude challenged the manager to provide irrefutable proof that Jason was unsuitable. It was agreed that Jason would also be assessed to establish some objective measure of potential. The assessment results proved that Jason had great potential to work at higher levels of complexity and demonstrated great leadership potential. Jason's manager was unable to counter the assessment findings with any tangible proof of unsuitability. Jason was nominated as a successor and developed for the financial manager role. The senior manager took a personal interest and requested ongoing developmental reports from Jason's manager to remove any signs of discrimination.

The next critical bias is the **blind spot bias**, where the HR facilitator or Line Manager is unaware of their own personal biases. This is detrimental to the succession process as the discussion will not be facilitated to ensure that employees' developmental areas and strengths are equally weighed.

The HR facilitator had experienced a conflict with Natasha, the Operations Manager. After a heated argument they had agreed to keep their disparate views of each other and adopted a professional working relationship of few verbal exchanges and more email communication. Natasha was unpopular in the department and many viewed her critical style as negative. When Natasha was discussed in the talent review, the HR facilitator's dislike for Natasha unknowingly influenced her facilitation style. She allowed more time for the managers that disliked Natasha to air their views and curtailed those that had positive feedback. The facilitator's personal bias towards Natasha meant that there was a skewed perception formed of Natasha that supported the HR manager's view.

Another bias is **stereotyping bias.** This is about making assumptions about an individual based on general impressions of a group of people. This generalisation often leads to unfair treatment of an individual.

Mishka was a hardworking employee with two young children. She worked flextime so that she could spend the afternoons with her children. Mishka had a reputation for consistent delivery and her contribution and loyalty were often praised. During the talent session, when Mishka was discussed from a potential perspective, there were unfair remarks made about her suitability as a successor. One manager felt that Mishka had two young children who would require her full attention; as a mother she would not be able to dedicate more time for her career. No career conversation was held with Mishka to determine her values and aspirations; the entire discussion was formed on baseless assumptions. Since Mishka was a young mother, she was stereotyped into the age old gender stereotype. The Line Manager was asked to engage Mishka in a proper career conversation and contrary to the assumptions, Mishka's husband ran his business from home and provided the necessary stability and support that allowed Mishka to actively pursue her career aspirations. Mishka was therefore reconsidered and placed on the succession plan.

The next bias is the **bandwagon effect**, which is a psychological phenomenon in which people do something primarily because other people are doing it, regardless of their own beliefs, which they may ignore or override. The bandwagon effect is the phenomenon of spreading certain beliefs among people of a group, community, country, etc., based on the following condition or rule - *the possibility of a belief being accepted by an individual rises if a large number of people have accepted it.*[13] So if many people perceive an employee will be a great successor, the manager may jump on the bandwagon and agree with this view even if he originally thought differently. The bandwagon effect is almost the adverse of the confirmation bias; with the bandwagon effect people change their minds too quickly in order to agree with the consensus opinion.

Thando was a new manager and he was struggling to fit in. The rest of the management had worked together for the past seven years and had a great comradery. Unlike the other managers who were all golf fanatics, Thando was more a squash enthusiast and understood little golf. These disparate interests created further division between Thando and his colleagues. Thando felt like a social outcast in the team and often went out of his way to earn respect from his colleagues. In his first talent review with the team, this social dynamic was evident. Every time the team voiced an opinion on someone, Thando surrendered his views and opinions to the team. This continued through most of the session until Thando's manager threw a spanner in the works and took Thando's opinion against the rest of the team. This gave Thando courage to maintain his opinions and the dynamics of the session shifted.

Choice supportive bias is the tendency for a decision-maker to defend his own decision or to later rate it better than it was, simply because he made it. I have often seen Line Managers stubbornly adhere to their view because it was their view and no amount of contradictory evidence can sway them.

Tanja was a brilliant lawyer and her track record for winning cases was celebrated in the organisation. This winning streak meant that Tanja felt that she was always right and her team had stopped challenging her. She was slowly developing a reputation for becoming stubborn and closed to any form of feedback. In the talent review session, Tanja's need to be right meant that whenever her view of her people was challenged, she would listen and then disregard all feedback. It was only when Tanja's manager challenged her on the high turnover of people in her department and her corresponding arrogant attitude, that Tanja slowly started to accept constructive feedback.

The **halo effect** is a type of unconscious bias in which our overall impression of a person influences how we feel and think about his or her character. Essentially, your overall impression of a person who you think is clever could lead you to make other assumptions about the person, such as that he is high-potential talent. The halo effect is the most common bias that Line Managers demonstrate when discussing high-potential employees.

Peter was a technical specialist who was brilliant at his work. He was also passionate about socio-economic development and actively volunteered for organisational projects like charity drives, however his leadership potential was limited. He was not a team player and often preferred projects which meant he could work alone. Yet due to Peter's high profile in the organisation, he was popular amongst the executives; it was assumed that Peter had great leadership potential and was nominated as a successor for a General Manager role. However once Peter was assessed, the assessment results confirmed the initial view.

EXAMPLE STATEMENTS DEMONSTRATING BIAS

Confirmation Bias
"Tell me I'm right."

Choice Supportive Bias
"It is the right choice because I made it."

Stereotyping Bias
"He is an accountant therefore he is a quiet person."

Bandwagon Effect
"I agree with all of you. Everyone can't be wrong."

Halo Effect
"Of course it means he is good at everything."

Blind Spot Bias
"I have no biases to anyone."

Indicators of a unhealthy succession management culture

▪ The names on the succession plan change each year. (There is a general lack of consistency and commitment to identified successors. Successors fall out of favour very easily.)

▪ No identified 'ready now' successors for critical roles. (There is a historical track record of the 'ready now' category being blank. This also demonstrates no progression on filling the talent pipeline.)

▪ The same successor is identified for many roles. (There are a few names that are attached to many different roles. This may indicate favouritism of a few over the many and that there is an insufficient number of employees to realistically provide succession coverage.)

▪ Sometimes successors are guaranteed roles when the organisation knows that these roles might not exist in the future.

▪ Successors identified as 'ready in one to two years' stay in that category year after year. (This demonstrates that these employees have not been developed to move to a 'ready now' category.)

- The succession is not in line with the transformation agenda. (The identified successors are not aligned to the organisation's employment equity plan which can potentially undermine progress made on achieving transformation targets.)

- There is no development budget available for successor development. (Apart from the ongoing development of employees, there is no additional development budget allocated for ensuring the readiness of successors.)

- The turnover of identified successors is extremely high. (If the turnover of the identified successors is extremely high this can indicate symptoms of bigger challenges in the organisations. There are insufficient opportunities for high-potential employees who are frustrated and leave.)[14]

- There is no focused development plan for successors aligned with their future roles. (Successors are developed but development goals are not aligned to the succession plan. This results in unprepared successors who are not ready for the next role.)

- Successors are not aware that they are on a succession plan. (This indicates a poor trust in the culture of the organisation. If successors are not informed that they are on a succession plan then no further development is done.)

- Certain critical positions have been vacant for more than six months which questions the validity and reliability of a succession plan. (The succession plan is obviously not effective and working.)

- The organisation has low turnover with insufficient opportunities for high-potential employees as there is no mobility of people or available vacancies. (These high–potential employees are not properly engaged and succession is reduced to identification only.)

- Successors' remuneration is not in line with market benchmarks and the organisation refuses to introduce addition retention incentives for this identified pool.

- The indiscriminate inclusion of successors on the succession plan questions the credibility of the entire process and devalues the high-potential employees who should be included.

Summary

- You can either choose an off-the-shelf succession process to implement in your organisation, or develop a customised process based on your organisational needs.

- If you select an off-the-shelf product then there are a few considerations to be made.

- If you choose to design your own approach then there are some guidelines you can choose to follow.

- There are numerous people challenges to succession that need to be identified and properly addressed.

- Succession is an emotionally charged topic and may lead to subjectivity. These emotions can sway logic and negatively influence succession outcomes.

- There are indicators of an unhealthy succession management culture that reflect the state of succession in the organisation.

Chapter 7

Succeeding at succession management

....

> *There are important considerations when planning for success,*
>
> *Are you satisfied with good enough or do you want to be the best?*
>
> *Is there a learning culture that facilitates employee growth?*
>
> *When deciding on the successor, who gets to vote?*
>
> *Critical success factors are key ingredients that you must include.*
>
> *Factors like transparency, communication and the frequency of successor reviews.*
>
> *To manage resistance, be prepared, don't just take a chance.*
>
> *Formulate responses to difficult questions well in advance.*

Now that we have reviewed the implementation process, we need to cover the essential ingredients that will make implementation a success. However, I would first like to share a hypothetical scenario to highlight that the apparent simplicity of succession management often comes with hidden levels of complexity.

Hypothetical scenario

As part of a challenge you were asked to bake a 50th birthday cake for a close friend who was having a huge birthday party with many esteemed guests. This was as a result of you boasting that you can become an expert just by watching YouTube videos. Your friend knows you have never baked a cake before but is prepared to give you an opportunity to prove her wrong. In her mind she trusts you will not let her down and assumes it is an easy task that you can master like all the other complex things you are great at doing. Knowing that this is very important and that it is a milestone birthday, you don't want to disappoint her and take it into your stride. You get a great recipe from the internet for a flop proof sponge cake. You are nervous but you think 'What can possibly go wrong?' You download a YouTube video and you are confident of your assured success. You do a trial run a month before the birthday party and the cake flops; it resembles a hard scone rather than any cake you have ever tasted. Frustrated you try a few more times and get the same result. You are desperate and consult with an expert Chef and you get asked a series of questions such as whether the flour was fresh, whether the oven was preheated, whether the ingredients were measured exactly, the temperature of the oven, the time period that the cake was baked in the oven, the working condition of the oven, the length of time you took to beat the cake batter, whether you opened the oven door whilst the cake was baking? You start to realise that baking a cake is much more difficult than getting a recipe off the internet. None of this information was included in the recipe. The Chef provides some basic advice on what you should and should not do. The next time you try baking the cake, it is an amazing improvement.

If you took this scenario and applied it to succession management, you would begin to see the similarities. Getting information and theories of succession processes off the internet may seem a contemporary thing to be doing, however the true test is in the implementation. There are many variables to be considered that will influence the effectiveness of your implementation. Below are the critical success factors that should be considered.

Critical success factors

Critical success factors can depend on your business context. Some variables may not be necessary whilst others may be non-negotiable. Review the following critical success factors and identify the ones that are critical to your organisation.

1. There must be **defined responsibilities and accountabilities**.

   Whilst the CEO may view succession management as part of her core responsibility to ensure a leadership pipeline to sustain and grow the organisation for the future governance of the enterprise, the ongoing sustainability and success of this practice lies with the HR executive. The HR executive has to position the business case, the framework and the process, and leverage the various HR disciplines and respective HR specialists to work in an integrated manner. The continuous implementation of this practice is the role of the managers.

2. The effectiveness of succession rests with the **ability to effortlessly synchronise different HR practices**.

   HR practices (talent planning, recruitment, career aspirations, coaching and mentorship, talent mobility, leadership development, and continuous assessment of readiness and engagement) need to integrate in a relatively seamless way to support the succession management practice. This means co-operation amongst the different HR specialists to contribute value to their respective areas of expertise.

3. Create a **learning culture to enable success in succession**.

   Create a learning culture in the organisation where employees have developed a positive habit of information and knowledge sharing. This practice is reinforced in the organisational culture and performance management, recognition and reward processes. For succession management to succeed, managers should embrace a willingness to share experience and skills. If this is embedded in the culture it becomes a business as usual practice.

4. There has to be **total objectivity in the succession management process**.

    The selection process must be based on a range of criteria, which are evaluated objectively against predetermined measures through various methods to ensure reliability of information. Fairness of this process in terms of proper identification, development and recruitment is critical to ensure the sustainability of the succession management strategy.

5. Successors **drive their own development**.

    Whilst the organisation will set up the infrastructure by implementing policies, processes and a framework to ensure a proper succession management process, the onus is on the individual to participate fully by initiating self-development and self-improvement initiatives that will enhance their own future success. The candidates in the talent pools must also be aware of their own career paths and there should be a level of ownership in the process.

6. The succession plan must **support the organisation's future strategic objectives and values.**

    If the focus is only on current roles without any consideration for the shift in business strategy, then the organisation is focused on replacement planning. There has to be alignment to the organisation's future core capabilities and future skill requirements in critical roles.

7. **Communicate succession plans to successors**.

    High-potential talent resign because they were not aware they were on a succession list. I have unfortunately seen this scenario play out time and time again in my career. When successors are eventually engaged and told it is usually too late, and they have psychologically checked out of the organisation. Therefore, once successors are identified and validated, they have to be informed. Communicating to successors in talent pools is necessary and provides legitimacy if they are visible in the organisation; it gives these individuals confidence that the organisation is serious about its investment in them and assists in the transition process to new roles. It is important to further back up this intention with support for their individual development plans and show commitment to reviewing their progress.

8. **Shift the focus** from planning for succession to developing the successors.

    A proportionally larger time is spent on the identification of successors than their development. Many organisations focus on formulating succession plans and very little time on the actual development of successors to create readiness. This is like spending a huge amount of time researching and planning a diet rather than actually actioning the plan and losing the weight.

9. **Understand and manage the culture** of the organisation.

    As previously discussed, culture can gradually annihilate all succession efforts if it is not understood and managed. When organisations have a low trust culture, confidentiality in the succession list is key. Even the most deserving successors who were chosen after a rigorous succession process will be subjected to scrutiny and discarded as "perceived favourites". There has to be significant work done on the culture to build trust once more. Transparency in terms of the succession process is key to building credibility, however it may take some time to achieve a high level of trust and transparency.

10. **Negotiate for sufficient time** with executives to implement the process and create a shared mindset about succession in the organisation.

I have seen succession initiatives fail on a colossal scale because the succession process was rushed to prove to key stakeholders that there was a credible succession process in place and that succession management was easily implementable. In the haste to commence with the process, the critical steps of communication and creating a common language around succession were overlooked.

11. **Linking of business strategy to succession.**

Succession management sessions should start with the business strategy as the context. Without the business strategy, the succession exercise becomes a superficial tick box exercise. The business strategy provides a depth of understanding of the people issues, especially the gaps in the relevant capabilities needed to take the business forward. The organisation's business strategy provides context for the succession discussion and there has to be constant alignment to shifting business priorities and corresponding talent requirements. Succession does not happen in a vacuum.

12. **Executive sponsorship** and support is a prerequisite.

The view often adopted in organisations about succession is that it is "much ado about nothing". Some leaders have the view that they are immortal in their roles, therefore concepts such as succession are great only as a tick box exercise to demonstrate to the Board that succession plans are in place. They perceive that there are more important business objectives to focus on right now. The problem with this mindset is that the very people you are trying to get to champion the practice see it as an obstacle to their ongoing tenure. There are numerous examples that come to mind where executives delayed decisions that directly impacted them. If the Chief Executive sponsors the process, he inadvertently provides his stamp of approval, lends credibility to the process, and will hold his executives accountable for any derailing of the process. This is a critical factor in rolling out almost all new practices, however this is especially true of succession, since there is a direct impact on organisational success and future sustainability. In Annexure 11 there are examples of the sorts of messages that must be weaved into the CEO's communication that demonstrates his personal support.

Two competitor organisations were in the process of implementing succession management. In the first organisation, the CEO was recently appointed and was at a level 1 succession. He was happy that there were identified successors for his executives. The succession process was limited to a list of names. No conversations happened and succession as a practice was never embraced to its full potential. The impact on the organisation was that it was more difficult to build a pipeline of leadership talent since there was no burning platform. In the second organisation, the CEO was longer in his role and he sanctioned that succession be cascaded to the top critical roles. The succession process was properly planned for annually. The succession conversation was linked to the business strategy, there was proper governance for the succession process, and it had greater acceptability in the organisation.

13. **Governance is fundamental**.

Governance of the succession process ensures process integrity. This can be done through centralised control over processes with a subject matter expert or talent specialist who creates and executes the succession strategy across the organisation. In large organisations this can be decentralised to individual business units which are responsible for their own succession management. The third option is a hybrid approach where the centralised talent specialist focuses on the senior roles and the junior critical roles are managed by business functions. The choice of these options depends on the structure of the organisation.

14. Establish **credibility** as the succession champion.

It is essential that if you are spearheading succession in the organisation you have an impeccable record for implementing and embedding processes. You should also have a track record for ethical conduct so that you are respected and trusted with sensitive succession documents. Sometimes the succession champion is a lonely role, where you need to play 'Devil's Advocate' and challenge the unconscious bias apparent in business. It is therefore important that you are seen as an objective party that has the organisation's best interests at heart.

15. Use **change management** to drive a talent mindset.

For succession management to become integral to your organisation, there has to be an adoption of the process and practice. There should also be a shift in the mindset or understanding of the characteristics of talent. To assist in this endeavour, there are many change management methodologies available which can be used to support the implementation and embedding of succession management. I have used the principles of the Prosci ADKAR model,[15] which ensures that risks are timeously identified and mitigated, issues are averted and stakeholders are engaged. The result will be a successful initiative.

16. Adopt **simple processes** that can be replicated.

HR is often accused of developing best practice complex processes that are great from an academic standpoint but have little business application. You can develop the best succession management process, but it means very little unless it is understood and implemented by your Line Managers. The execution of the process should be so basic that any Line Manager can understand the key concepts and the process for a flawless implementation. This will enhance the efficiency and sustainability of the process.

17. Ensure succession **process integrity**.

Process integrity refers to the consistency of the process and whether all role players apply the process in the same way and have the same understanding of definitions. This prevents a waste of time and effort when individuals are incorrectly categorised as high potential by some and discounted by others because the criteria are inconsistently applied. This questions the credibility of the process.

18. Line Managers should **prepare adequately** for the succession review.

    When Line Managers attend succession review sessions and have not adequately prepared, this creates real frustration amongst other business leaders who have taken the time to read the necessary documents and complete the correct templates. This also disadvantages the employees who are discussed and diminishes the value of the session.

19. **Correct representation** in the talent review committee meetings.

    Appropriate business leaders need to be present in the meetings to provide value to the discussion. When the right people are in the session then there are robust discussions and traditional stereotypes or biases are challenged. This provides a more reliable outcome. I have had numerous experiences in talent review sessions where the wrong level of leaders were included; they did not contribute value to the conversation and often had very little insight into the employees being discussed, so they held up the flow of the discussion by asking questions for their own understanding rather than contributing to the discussion.

20. **Generational succession** is a reality so understand the dynamics.

    The reality is that Baby Boomers are close to retirement and suddenly there are four generations in an organisation, each of which is characterised by a unique approach to work and different expectations about the psychological contract of work. These dynamics must be considered when looking at the different ages and expectations of successors.

21. **Managing risks in succession**.

Research done by the Corporate Leadership Council (2003) demonstrates that organisations that are most effective at succession management have successfully managed four risks (vacancy, readiness, transition and portfolio risk) to the leadership support chain.[16]

Vacancy risk

The key risk that organisations encounter is the departure or absence of key talent. These organisations continually use analytics to ensure that succession management safeguards the business capabilities needed for strategy achievement. An integrated succession management process that is embedded in an organisation can effectively address vacancy risk by ensuring suitable successors are identified, developed and equipped to transition into vacant roles.

Readiness risk

This refers to the risk of underdeveloped successors who are not ready for transitioning into a vacant role. This is often caused by organisations not actively managing the development of successors and reviewing their progress in achieving developmental goals. Talent review committees will determine the readiness and suitability of successors to specific roles through ongoing assessments.

Transition risk

This refers to the assimilation of talent into the organisation. Even where successors appear ready to fill senior positions, a number of people fail soon after succession occurs. This relates to other factors such as insufficient support to succeed in the role. Organisations can decide that only once these potential successors have been through the appropriate development, are ready to take on additional responsibility and work at a higher level of complexity, will they considered for the new position.

To ensure a smooth transition to the new role, successors can be exposed to job rotation, job shadowing and acting in the position.

Portfolio risk

This refers to the risk of poor deployment of talent against business goals and highlights the poor matching of the right people to the right roles. This is a dynamic process and can be addressed by the talent review committees, who will focus on refining and matching the succession talent to the changing business strategy.

Frequently Asked Questions

In highlighting the critical success factors, I tried to include additional variables that should be considered. Just as important is being prepared for a surplus of questions once succession management is launched in your organisation. You need to understand your organisational context and prepare for questions that may arise directly as well as indirectly as a result of succession. I have included common generic questions often posed by HR practitioners.

1. **What if employees are distraught that they are not identified as a successor?**

    Succession may be perceived as the coveted golden egg by some employees, who may become disappointed and then disengaged if they are not selected as part of a talent pool. This situation has to be managed quickly with the employee and the Line Manager needs to have a one-on-one discussion with them to realistically review the employee's knowledge and abilities. The embedding of career conversations in the organisation can assist Line Managers to deal with these emotional responses. The above scenario should be built into your succession training session with Line Managers.

2. **Do I roll out succession management to all levels in the organisation? When do I use career management?**

Succession is used for critical roles, however some organisations cascade to junior roles and this becomes more focused career management.

3. **What information is it necessary to obtain in a career conversation?**

Career conversations are necessary as there is relevant information that a manager must acquire to determine future succession fits. Performance discussions are usually focused on the performance contract and development plan; there is often little time to discuss information that is more of a personal nature such as values, expectations, mobility and career aspirations. The career conversation is therefore an ideal time to determine this information.

In national and international companies, possible vacancies may be in other geographic locations, so it is necessary to find out if an employee can be redeployed or if there are any personal constraints like family commitments which may prevent them from relocating.

4. **Do I Implement career management or succession management first or in tandem?**

It is better to implement career management first in the organisation, however if there is an urgent need for succession, then roll out career conversations as part of the succession process as this enables a basic understanding of employees' career aspirations. Then plan around implementing proper career management.

5. **How do you ensure that the incumbent manager has sufficiently transferred knowledge and wisdom?**

You need to test if knowledge was suitably passed on, as well as get feedback from the successor. There are different options to ensure this happens, for example incentivise your managers with remuneration if they coach and mentor their successors and prepare them for the new role. You can also build it into a manager's Key Performance Indicators and link it to their performance bonus.

6. **How do I address a low attrition rate?**

The reality is that there are blocked pipelines in organisations due to the poor economy in South Africa presently; employees are too afraid to search for new jobs in other organisations as a result of the Last In First Out principle. One solution may be that managers who are close to retirement age could consider early retirement as an incentive, however this depends on whether organisations can afford it.

7. **Generation Y successors are ambitious and are waiting for opportunities. How do you deal with their expectations?**

Deal honestly with their expectations. You need to become creative by giving them exposure, for example providing access to leadership initiating recognition events such as breakfast with the CEO. Do not ignore them or you will lose them to your competitors.

8. **What about employees with five years to retirement who are cruising along?**

This is indicative of a poor performance culture and poor consequence management. Use your performance management process to actively manage their annual deliverables and build in mentorship goals. These managers must have identified successors who will be assessed regularly on their receipt of knowledge and experience.

9. **What factors might prevent an employee from being selected as a successor?**

Some considerations why someone may not be selected as a successor include:

- Limited capability.

- Psychological blocks.

- Close to retirement.

- The employee's race is not in line with the transformation plan.

- Engagement level.

- Performance track record is poor.

- Poor culture fit.

- Limited leadership potential.

- Emotional immaturity.

- General personality derailers, e.g. arrogance.

10. **How do I handle identified successors who are part of a talent pool but do not get the identified role?**

Do not create expectations with any of the successors; they are part of a pool of successors and should have met all the succession conditions that were contracted with them. They need to be aware of what the selection criteria are to be appointed as a successor.

11. **How do I know if successors are ready for a role?**

Track their development on a regular basis. There are various 360-degree assessments you can do to evaluate their readiness level. The success of the projects they were managing could be another indicator.

12. **How do I deal with managers' feelings of insecurities?**

This is usually when managers are stuck and have no envisaged view of the future. You need to establish a coaching relationship with these managers to shift their perceptions and they need to develop a level of personal mastery. Enroll them in a career workshop that helps them gain a deeper understanding of their self. Converting these dissenters to succession advocates takes time. You know you are successful when they become your biggest advocates. Remember behavioural change takes time; these managers need to be guided to reconnect with the meaning in their roles.

- Various critical factors were discussed in the chapter that exponentially enhance the implementation of success.

- Frequently Asked Questions indicate whether all planning is comprehensively done or whether there are still outstanding issues that need to be covered.

Chapter 8

Managing successor transition into vacant roles

When the fruit ripens on the branch, the tree bows down,

The mentor kneels with humility to the ground.

The moment of truth has finally arrived,

When moved into the new role, can the successor thrive?

Did the successor make sufficient developmental progress?

Is the successor suitably set up for success?

What was considered when selecting from the talent pool?

Was it the most promising person or the one that transcended the rules?

Is the challenge really what the successor sought?

Is there a network in place to provide support?

Is there a culture fit with the team in the new role?

Does the successor feel he reached his aspired career goal?

This poem aptly describes that when the successor is ready for transition into the new role, the manager kneels down in humility and reverence after passing the baton. However the story does not end here. You may have followed all the correct steps to implementation and have robust high-potential talent, however only once the successor has successfully transitioned into the role and is contributing effectively can success be celebrated. The succession transition process can be riddled with difficulty when certain factors are not considered. To illustrate this point I am going to share the lessons I learnt through my brief gardening experience.

Two years ago I was determined to transform my garden and create a more conducive environment for relaxation and reflection. My daughter was one and I thought of designing a conducive place for play, so I enthusiastically searched on Google for the prettiest flowers to create a breathtaking environment. My knowledge of gardening was unfortunately non-existent. I thought, 'How difficult could it be? Just purchase the plants that are required and get a gardener to transplant them into pots'. So off I went to spend a small fortune on a variety of different blossoming plants. In theory it sounded like an easy endeavour, but in practice it was the beginning of a series of great life lessons. I know now what the idiom 'A little knowledge is a dangerous thing' means. Without consulting with any authority on understanding the nature of plants or even reading a dummies guide to gardening, I made the assumption that plants are independent and that they genetically know what to do to thrive. I could just decide what I wanted based on the colours and the fragrance of the flowers. I had no other criteria as I wasn't aware of what other criteria would be critical.

Lesson 1

"When in doubt, consult the expert". Read up and discover what information is necessary. Do not take things at face value. Sometimes the best intentions have unintended consequences. When you introduce something which you perceive will be of value to employees, establish facts through the employees themselves rather than making assumptions. In the context of succession, always strive to understand the successors in the talent pool.

A month after the plants were in my garden, I noticed that whilst some were flourishing, others were not doing very well. Not all plants are equal; there is a level of diversity and they grow in different environments. I had assumed all plants love the sun and so placed them directly in the light, only to find that I had placed many shade plants in the sun and the environment was not conducive to their growth.

Lesson 2

Understand the environment and what is required before deploying successors into roles. Understanding the environment in a business arena could mean evaluating the business maturity, culture and the dynamics of existing teams. There has to be a fit to the job, but more importantly a fit to the team; different leadership styles are required in different team environments.

The next thing I did was water these plants daily, since water was the only nourishment they were getting. It became a habit to get home after work, walk in the garden and water my plants. I was feeling very proud of myself in the discipline I was exercising, only to find the surprising feedback I was getting was the wilting of my beautiful lavender plants. So I researched and found certain plants are more resilient and that too much water can have a detrimental effect and actually kill the plant.

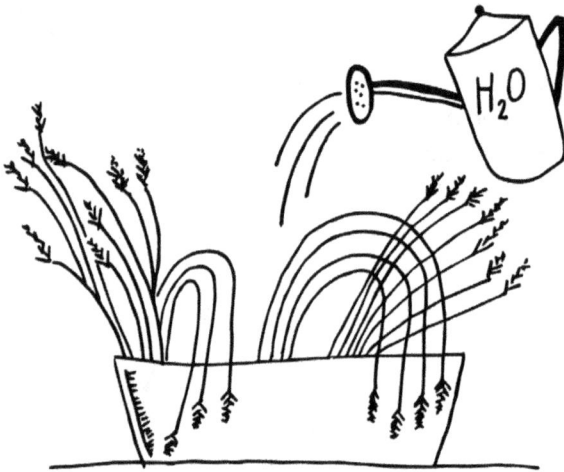

Lesson 3

Understand that people, like plants, are different, with different values that differentiate and motivate them. Do not make assumptions; what you think motivates someone may actually have the opposite effect. It is important to take the time to understand employee differences; too much attention leads to stunted leadership and creates a dependency. There has to be sufficient room available to make decisions and to acquire wisdom through exercised judgement and experience.

In the first year, using the two fundamental lessons, I persevered in my passion for gardening. All went well until winter arrived, and I found that not all my beautiful plants survived. As I watched my investment diminish, I learnt yet another lesson. The plants that I had purchased were biennial, i.e. they only last for a short period. What I should have bought were perennial plants. The definition of perennial is lasting or existing for a long or apparently infinite time, enduring or continually recurring.

Lesson 4

I learnt that all that glitters is not gold. The plants that survived were not the ones with the prettiest flowers, but the shrubs that were most hardy. Similarly, we may be impressed with employees who appear to be ticking all the boxes regarding their CV and track record, but after a while they lose steam and what initially impressed you about them appear to be superficial qualities and not the resilience, agility and grit that are required from employees in a new work context. Rather spend the extra time and money to determine the true calibre of employees who can thrive in your organisation. This can be achieved by an integrated selection process of interviews and valid and reliable assessment.

When I looked at my plants post winter I realised that other seedlings had started to grow in the same plant. I was unsure what to do. Do I leave them in or do I pull them out? This internal dialogue continued for a few weeks until my gardener innocently suggested that if I wanted healthy plants then I needed to remove the weeds. He pointed out that weeds rob the nutrition from flowers and need to be removed to allow plants space to grow properly. In my short stint as an amateur gardener I had not learnt how to identify the weeds.

Lesson 5

Sometimes counterproductive employees are behavioural outliers, who have to be identified and properly managed as they negatively impact the health of the organisation. In organisations there are many high maintenance employees who will divert your focus and drain your energy in managing them. They have a negative influence on the team, do not contribute any added value, and often divert attention from recognising those doing a good job. It is often better to deal effectively with these employees than expect them to miraculously turn over a new leaf.

Since I was open to his advice, my gardener proceeded to explain the importance of pruning existing plants; it is necessary to get rid of old offshoots which divert nutrition from the main plant. I absorbed the lessons in pruning and rushed off to apply my newfound knowledge.

Lesson 6

Successors have to be refined and groomed and sometimes need to be reminded that they are not peacocks but actually peahens. You do not want successors to experience entitlement issues. As soon as behaviours of entitlement surface they must be dealt with, as they can create a toxic culture and may be detrimental to the department.

During my gardening adventure, parts of South Africa started to experience water shortages as water levels continued to drop in the dams. Given the stringent water restrictions in most of South Africa, water as a precious resource needed to be conserved. I have adapted to these restrictions by using grey water so I can still devotedly water my plants.

Lesson 7

South Africa is presently going through difficult economic times, which has a direct effect on business performance and financial results. One of the first lines to get cut on a budget is unfortunately learning and development. So without sufficient financial resources, how do we ensure that successors are adequately prepared for roles? The answer is through creative experience and exposure.

As I was not sure where I wanted to plant them, I had left my plants in pots versus planting them in the ground, however as time passed the pots became too small for my growing plants.

| Lesson 8 | Successors in talent pools are more sensitive as they are between two worlds - their present jobs and their future possible roles. Keeping them too long in the succession pool means they will become restless and want to be given greater opportunities. |

Having learnt over two years from my gardening and management lessons, I was appreciating the fruits of my labour until I found out that my daughter had developed an allergy to bees. I was disappointed since I had really toiled over this initiative. This was my most profound lesson to date.

<table>
<tr><td>Lesson 9</td><td>Sometimes we start a project on a whim in organisations without doing proper due diligence or an impact analysis. On the surface what may seem like a great idea can often introduce other consequences. I know of an organisation that</td></tr>
</table>

introduced a graduate programme as it was what other organisations were doing. They invested a substantial amount of money in the initiative, but this created an uproar with existing employees whose morale was negatively impacted. The employees, many of whom were academically qualified, were displeased that the organisation had not invested in their development but had recruited external graduates to develop into manager roles. The lesson here is to conduct an impact analysis before you implement new processes.

I didn't really want to remove my beautiful plants as I had invested so much effort and time in growing and nurturing them, so I consulted with some experts and they suggested I place insect repellant plants close to the flowering plants to keep the bees away.

<table>
<tr><td>Lesson 10</td><td>Your succession practices could be quite successful where you tick all the right boxes, however your success could mean that there will be other organisations buzzing around your successors trying to entice them away. What would be your</td></tr>
</table>

equivalent plant that could retain these successors?

I had transplanted a healthy plant into another container, forgetting that the container did not have drainage for excess water. My innocent mistake destroyed the plant and caused the plant to rot from the roots.

Lesson 11

Similarly, when we transition successors into new environments, we need to check if the work that the employee deals with developmentally challenges or overwhelms them. Does the individual have sufficient support to deal with challenges? Is there continuous debriefing to prevent the successor from becoming overwhelmed and drowning? Introduce enough challenges to stimulate growth without stressing your successors.

In the two years since I started my gardening project, my plants have grown incrementally. There has been gradual development that I notice since I have been tracking their progress. My high expectations of having a beautiful flower garden is taking time to manifest.

Lesson 12

I liken implementing succession to planting a fruit tree; it takes years to mature. Time is required for the tree to grow roots and a strong foundation. Similarly, succession has to be embedded, with Line Managers and high-potentials trusting the process. The fruit in the case of succession are the available and ready successors waiting to be picked. You need to manage unrealistic expectations about the return of investment in succession.

Being a novice gardener, I am still learning from Mother Nature. I don't know everything about gardening, but I am keeping an open mind and I learn a little more every day.

Lesson 13

As a facilitator of succession in your organisation, there will always be people challenges and lessons you need to learn. It takes time to refine your skills, so be prepared to continuously learn and adapt to business strategy changes.

Building succession management sustainability

The build up to implementing succession management is like the build up to the New Year. Before the New Year everyone wants to make New Year's resolutions about what they are going to commit to. The clock strikes midnight and the dawning of a new era in the organisation. There are exalted shouts of celebration and a lot of congratulations and patting of backs. By 2am the excitement of a new year dwindles as people start to yawn, and the revelers call it a night. The huge milestone everyone was waiting for has now passed and some of the excitement and energy has significantly declined. It is such an anticlimax.

So too are the emotions with succession. You have done a whole lot of pre-work. You have run the first succession process. You have delivered an amazing process. Successors have been identified and validated, and individual development plans are in place. So now what? How do you maintain the excitement and momentum to succession? What about the resolutions that were made at the onset? How do you action those resolutions?

The following points refer to other factors that can impact succession sustainability in your organisation, and it is necessary to bear it in mind when it happens. Sometimes there are factors outside your control that will determine the success and effectiveness of the practice.

Throwing out the baby with the bath water

New business leaders or new HR leaders who join the organisation often position the need to change. New people in an organisation want to prove their contribution through the rewriting of processes under the disguise of process improvement. They often bring along templates from previous organisations because they are familiar and comfortable with them. The challenge is to manage their ideas and suggestions by listening to improvements with an openness. If there are great ideas or suggestions, incorporate them into the work that is being done without throwing out all the hard work and starting from the beginning again. Do not underestimate the level of acceptance of succession in the business; by introducing a new process, you are placing a reset switch where you need to do all the hard work of creating readiness again, mitigating risks and dealing with resistance. It is easier to refine existing processes and gradually introduce changes than making bold announcements of a brand new succession process. This may only be applicable if the existing succession process is rife with perceived favouritism and has a reputation for inequitable practices.

Examining whether the baton was in fact effectively passed on

Mitigating possible risks is like putting a new roof on your house – you may follow the perfect process and buy the best materials in the market, but at the onset of the first storm and downpour, will that new roof be able to withstand the tenacious force of nature or will it succumb to the first torrent of rain? Unfortunately you may never know until it rains. Similarly, in succession, the correct processes may be followed but the true test is when a vacancy exists and the question is raised as to whether there is a 'ready now' successor. How easy is the transition into the vacant post? Is the successor capable of dealing with the demands of the new role easily? Can they make the correct decisions required at that level? Does the person seamlessly integrate with the business operation? Can she take the reins of leadership without hesitation?

Que sera sera (what will be, will be)

As I browse through my LinkedIn profile, I cannot help but ponder over the senior people in my contacts who have recently joined different organisations in more senior roles. What was the state of succession in their previous organisations? Were they part of a succession plan, in a talent pool, or not flagged as talent at all? Given the evolving nature of executive recruitment which comprises additional bars to jump over, it is no easy feat to be appointed to these roles, which leads me to believe that they were in a talent pool. So why did they leave? The simple truth is that no matter how dynamic and brilliant your organisation, there will still be an element of challenge offered by another organisation purely because it offers something new, unpredictable and therefore intriguing. We need to continually evolve our skills to ensure relevance. The mature response is that they are regrettable losses, but at least they are adding value to another organisation and contributing to the wider society and country.

When life happens

Engagement and retention have to be considered when implementing succession management; you may have the most effective succession identification and development process, but there is no guarantee that successors will stay. You may argue that you have great incentive schemes in place, however sadly life happens.

In one of the organisations I worked at there was a high-potential employee with great potential. He was a star performer and fully engaged in the organisation. He had been in the organisation for five years and he was told he was part of a succession plan. There was already a sufficient amount of budget invested in his development. The risk of him leaving was pretty low and the certainty of him transitioning into the next leadership role was a given. Unfortunately a tragedy struck where his home was broken into, and the traumatic experience was the catalyst that made him emigrate to another country. Having young children, he placed their safety ahead of his career ambition.

Influencing the flow of turnover in talent pools

Sometimes you may have the best culture and a great employee value proposition, but employees still leave. The aim is not to be obsessed about generic organisation turnover but rather to focus on turnover within a talent pool. There will always be an expected level of attrition - the trick is to be able to influence the flow rather than to try and totally stop the attrition.

The ripple effect of succession

The transition of successors into a new role is a well-choreographed dance with different transitions and moves, but every move is in tandem with the beat of the music. Sometimes the rhythm is relatively slow and dancing is done at a slower pace enabling dancers to accomplish their dance moves with a greater precision. However the quality of the performance deteriorates when there is an erratic rhythm with unrehearsed dancers. It is important that every dance move is properly rehearsed. Some dancers come on stage while others go off stage, and there are those dance moves that require precision where one catches a dancer in the air. Timing is everything.

The above analogy can be applied to the choreographed transitions that happen in an organisation. As a successor fills a vacancy, his role becomes vacant and requires a successor. A succession process is only as effective as the number of successful transitions that successors make into new positions. Succession is about job shadowing and practice before moving into a vacant role. Like a well-choreographed dance, it is about all the dancers - one movement flows into the next.

Conditions of succession

You need to build in specific conditions of succession in your succession management policy. The following are some ideas you can consider. To determine the appointment of a successor into an identified role, at the time that an identified role becomes available, the following specific criteria will be considered:

- The position must still exist in the organisation even though it might have moved to another business area.
- The candidate has demonstrated a keenness to still be considered for the role.
- The candidate must be signed off as being competent or likely to be competent in a period of less than six months.

- If the candidate is not yet competent, he must demonstrate significant progress in his developmental plan.

- The outputs of the position should not have significantly changed.

- The candidate must have maintained a consistently high performance standard.

Summary

- This chapter focuses on the practice of transitioning successors into critical roles. It starts off by drawing succession lessons from my real life experience.

- The critical lessons applied to succession management were as follows:

  - **Lesson one:** "When in doubt, consult the expert". Read up and discover what information is necessary. Sometimes the best intentions have unintended consequences.

  - **Lesson two:** Understand the environment and the corresponding requirements before placing employees in vacant roles.

  - **Lesson three:** Understand that people are different, with different values that differentiate and motivate them.

  - **Lesson four:** Understand the real qualities of your employees, i.e. the resilience, agility and grit that are required in an ever changing work context.

- **Lesson five:** It is often more important to effectively deal with high maintenance employees than to expect them to miraculously turn over a new leaf.

- **Lesson six:** Successors have to be refined and groomed, and sometimes need to be reminded that they are not peacocks but actually peahens.

- **Lesson seven:** South Africa is presently going through difficult economic times which has a direct effect on business performance and financial results. Use limited financial resources to prepare successors adequately for roles.

- **Lesson eight:** Successors in talent pools are more impatient. Maintain their engagement levels to retain them.

- **Lesson nine:** Sometimes we start a project on a whim in organisations without doing proper due diligence or an impact analysis.

- **Lesson ten:** Your succession practices could be quite successful, however your success could mean that there will be other organisations buzzing around your successors trying to entice them away.

- **Lesson eleven:** When we transition successors into new environments, we need to check if the work that the employee deals with developmentally challenges or overwhelms them.

- **Lesson twelve:** Manage unrealistic expectations about the return of investment of succession as it takes a long time to mature.

- **Lesson thirteen**: As a facilitator of succession in your organisation there will be continuous people challenges and lessons you will learn. It takes time to refine your skills; be prepared to continuously learn and adapt to business strategy changes.

■ Some factors that impact succession sustainability will be outside of your control. That is the nature of the business.

Chapter 9

Success measures and metrics

Remember what gets measured, gets done...

If you cannot measure the impact on business results, then your succession efforts are in vain.

Repeating the same folly year after year is clearly bordering on insane.

When striving for excellence, measurement is key,

Has there been continuous improvement in the quality and quantity?

It is better to have received feedback, measured and failed,

Than be lulled by a false sense of security that your process is hailed.

Remember practice makes perfect as the idiom goes,

So dust off the criticism and use the business response to grow.

To measure or not to measure should never be a question for debate,

You have to quantify the impact of moving from one to another state.

There are many organisations that implement succession management and start to pop the champagne because it is the end of an arduous journey. I am in no way belittling this great milestone, however the celebrations should only start when you are positively improving on all the succession measures year upon year.

Process implementation

Measurement should occur on two levels - process implementation and actual talent metrics. The measurement of process implementation should be the one you complete first. You know you are successful when succession management is designed, developed, delivered, embraced, adopted and consistently used. This can be achieved through a feedback survey done with business. You can use the survey in Annexure 13 to assess the success of your process implementation.

It is important that you contract with the executives at the onset on the organisational succession metrics. Remember to measure against specific objectives. You need to be able to properly articulate the end goal. What will success look like? What will the tangible indicators of success be?

It is important to introduce basic measures at the beginning and when your succession process matures, you can introduce more sophisticated measures. You can include both qualitative and quantitative measures as part of your analytics.

Qualitative measures

A qualitative measure could be that the succession management process has been cascaded to different tiers in the organisation. In year one it could be at the executive level, year two could be at the senior management level, and year three could include critical roles at a middle management level. Another qualitative measure could be the level of exposure that successors are given through the initiative. Year one could be job shadowing, year two could be coaching and mentorship, and year three could be rotations and secondments. You can review which employees have moved from the 'ready in one to two years' to the 'ready now' category. You can also measure the progression of succession management from a purely manual paper-based process to an automated technology equipped solution that provides succession metrics in real time. You can measure the level of transparency in the culture over a period of time, and can look at whether Line Managers are more equipped to have career conversations over time.

Talent metrics: Succession coverage

Succession coverage is often the most common measurement used in succession management; it is something tangible that provides a quick scan of the current state of succession in your organisation. This can be the baseline measure against which you can track progress year after year. The ratio of succession coverage is determined by turnover of employees in the role. The senior roles can have a 3 to 1 succession coverage, which means that for every critical role there are three identified successors, however for roles where there is high turnover, it is important to have a higher succession coverage - maybe 5 to 1.

You can measure the percentage of succession coverage for the following roles:

- Percentage of successors in the 'ready now' category compared to those still needing additional years of further development. This metric reflects present succession bench strength.

- Percentage of successors in the 'emergency successor' category. This measure is a great indicator of the leadership culture in the organisation. The ability of Line Managers to identify emergency successors demonstrates their willingness to support the succession process. This is the easiest milestone that one can put in place.

- Percentage of successors in the 'ready in one to two years' category. Remember that for this category there should be a reduction in the percentage value after two years. If the same names appear it indicates no focused development was done with these successors.

- Percentage of successors in the 'ready in two to three years' category. This is a long term view and there is always a higher number of successors identified in this category. I have often found that there is a skewed perception by managers that more successors should be placed in this category over the others.

- Percentage of no succession coverage in total number of roles. This indicates the positions which present vacancy risk. This require a business decision to address the gap. This can also be in highly specialised roles where succession will most likely be sourced via an external pool.

Frequency of measurement

You need to track measures within a regular time period, which can be annually or biannually. In your first year you will get a baseline measure, which will hopefully improve over time as your succession practices are embedded. This provides a stake in the ground for where you are presently. The difficult work is maintaining momentum in the organisation; you need to play the custodian role of ensuring the process integrity of the succession process. This means making sure the correct process is followed and that correct criteria are used to identify successors in an ongoing process. You constantly need to onboard new managers into the process and mentor them on the responsibilities of their roles.

Diversity metrics

Apart from the generic succession metrics mentioned earlier in the chapter, it is imperative that diversity metrics are superimposed onto the generic succession information. The diversity metric tells a story of how committed the organisation is to transformation.

- The percentage of females in the total succession population who are identified successors for critical roles.
- The percentage of designated groups (Black, Coloured and Indian) of the total group who are identified as successors.
- The percentage of talent of the total succession population with disabilities.
- The percentage of successors from the designated group who have transitioned into critical roles.

Measuring succession movement

- The percentage of successors who are mobile if you work in a national or international business.

- The percentage of critical roles filled by identified successors over a 12 month period.

- The percentage of regretted departures of people who have left the organisation over a 12 month period.

- The attrition percentage of successors from the designated groups (Black, Coloured and Indian) over a 12 month period.

- Turnover rate of newly appointed successors in critical roles.

- Risk of leaving within the talent pool is a lead measure which can assist in proactively identifying areas of concern that should be addressed.

- Talent pool attrition rates are a lag measure. Attrition rates can reflect the effectiveness of the talent engagement and development strategy. As your succession practice improves, this attrition rate will gradually decrease.

Other measures that can be considered

- The percentage of difficult to fill roles compared to all other vacancies in the organisation. This information can be determined by a recruitment specialist who can provide the length of time that certain roles remain vacant.

- The percentage of employees presently in critical roles over 55 years of age. This is a lead indicator of possible vacancy risks that require 'ready now' successors.

- The ratio of internal to external talent placements in the organisation. This can also indicate the strength of an organisation's succession pool. If a high number of leaders are coming from external sources, it may be time to build a stronger pipeline of successors.

- The performance ratings curve of identified successors against the readiness of successors. This can reassure you that the identified successors in the talent pool are the correct individuals.

- The percentage of successors who have met their contracted development objectives in a 12 month period. This demonstrates the commitment and motivation of successors.

- Length of tenure of successors once appointed in a new critical role. This indicates whether all the necessary support was in place to assist the successor in his role.

Presenting statistics

Once you have calculated succession metrics, you need to convert these metrics into a succession dashboard that provides a visual representation of the information. This is usually used in executive feedback to track the progress of succession in the organisation. My experience is that the presentation of statistics in the form of graphs convinces them of the value of the exercise, and your credibility with your stakeholders subsequently also improves. The succession dashboard is represented in business language. This dashboard is often used in executive meetings and shared with the Board on the succession progress in the organisation.

summary

- *This chapter focused on success measures and metrics of succession.*

- *You can get general succession implementation feedback via a feedback form distributed in the organisation.*

- *The most common measure for succession is succession coverage for critical roles.*

- *There is a list of other measures you can review depending on your organisation's requirements.*

Chapter 10

Final words: To infinity and beyond

Parting words of wisdom...

Slow and steady is often believed to win the race,

In succession it is most definitely the case.

Follow the basic recipe once you have all the tools,

Remember to adopt foundational principles, just follow the basic rules.

Alas our apprenticeship is over, may your succession tree annually bear fruit,

With a growing leadership pipeline filled with surplus successors you can recruit.

Just consider all the critical variables and learn to crawl before you run.

Succession is really an arduous but rewarding journey when all is said and done.

In writing this book I am cognisant of the subtle irony that through this book I am practicing some of the principles of succession management by transferring knowledge and experience to you. There is an overwhelming feeling of both nostalgia and regret that we have to part ways dear HR practitioner. This book has given me the ability to reflect on the last two decades working in corporate South Africa. I may have shared too much information which may be overwhelming to you, however remember to break it down into manageable phases. Choose the knowledge that can best serve you in your exciting journey ahead.

Succession management is critical from a business continuity perspective, however an organisation cannot only focus telescopically on the future; it needs to pay attention to the present profitability of the business. That means focusing on all employees who drive business growth and revenue. Organisations depend on the strength of all employees irrespective of whether they are in critical roles. There are some individual contributors who remain committed to specialising and may never aspire to climb the rungs of succession. Their contribution to the business is immeasurable so you need to find appropriate ways to engage and retain them. It is essential that you have a comprehensive engagement strategy to drive a differentiated value strategy for this segment of employees.

Remember today's labour force has more generations working together than ever before, and there are various expectations on the path towards leadership positions. Do not make the assumption that everyone should be treated alike; treat people not how you like to be treated, but how they want to be treated. With digital acceleration and the continuous changing business landscape, you may be tempted to throw up your hands in resignation and wonder whether there is a point to succession when jobs are quickly becoming obsolete, however I implore you to consider that the reality in South Africa is that for this moment in time, succession is still very relevant and has a critical role to play in your business sustainability. Start the foundational work now rather than deferring it to a later time which may be too late.

Remember to silence the inner critic who will question your confidence and skills to implement succession. I have provided a map with possible potholes on the way, but I have also given some suggestions to avoid these potholes, so take my well-grounded advice and fly up, up and away...

ANNEXURES

Annexure 1: Readiness checklist

Checklist to assess readiness for implementation of responsive succession management in your organisation

		Not even close	Some way to go	Nearly there	We're there
A	**Organisational capacity** To what extent do you think:	0	1	2	3
A1	There is leadership support from top management in the form of a designated person responsible for implementation?				
A2	The organisation has a great track record in driving, implementing and embedding new processes.				
A3	The designated succession subject matter expert has designed a communication and change plan to implement succession.				
A4	There are financial resources allocated to the success of the implementation of this practice.				
A5	Succession will be given priority in line with other business priorities.				

B	**Functional considerations**	0	1	2	3
	To what extent do you think:				
B1	There is a HR system that can provide reliable employee data that can be used for the process.				
B2	A performance culture is driven in the organisation with performance feedback continuously shared.				
B3	Career management is embedded in the organisation.				
B4	The HR team is well trained and able to implement and sustain the succession management practice.				
B5	The HR team understands the knowledge and has the skills required to facilitate robust succession discussions.				

C	**Functional considerations**	0	1	2	3
	To what extent do you think:				
C1	There is a high level of trust in leadership in the organisation.				
C2	There is an embedded culture of transparency and communication between management and employees.				
C3	Managers are known for driving development in their teams.				
C4	There are developmental opportunities available for staff to pursue.				

C5 There is defined accountability to make the succession management practice successful.

D **Senior leadership support**

To what extent do you think:

	0	1	2	3

D1 Senior leadership understands the business continuity risk of not having a succession management process.

D2 Senior leadership is mature enough to select successors based on the needs of the organisation.

D3 Senior leadership is willing and able to lead and shape the implementation.

D4 Senior leadership and management inculcate a learning culture that is encouraged.

D5 Senior leadership is committed to creating a robust succession management practice.

E **Employee readiness**

To what extent do you think:

	0	1	2	3

E1 Continuous growth and development is desired by employees.

E2 Employees are open to new HR processes and practices.

E3 Employees understand the practice of succession in the organisation.

E4 Employees have career conversations with their Line Managers.

E5 Employees take ownership for driving their careers.

Add the totals for each section and plot them along the appropriate line. Connect the dots and a web will emerge which will highlight areas that require work within your organisation.

Total Readiness Score	
	Score
Organisational capacity	
Functional considerations	
Organisational culture	
Senior leadership support	
Employee readiness	

Total Readiness Score

Organisational
Capacity
15

10

5

0

Employee
Readiness

Functional
Considerations

Senior
Leadership
Support

Organisational
Culture

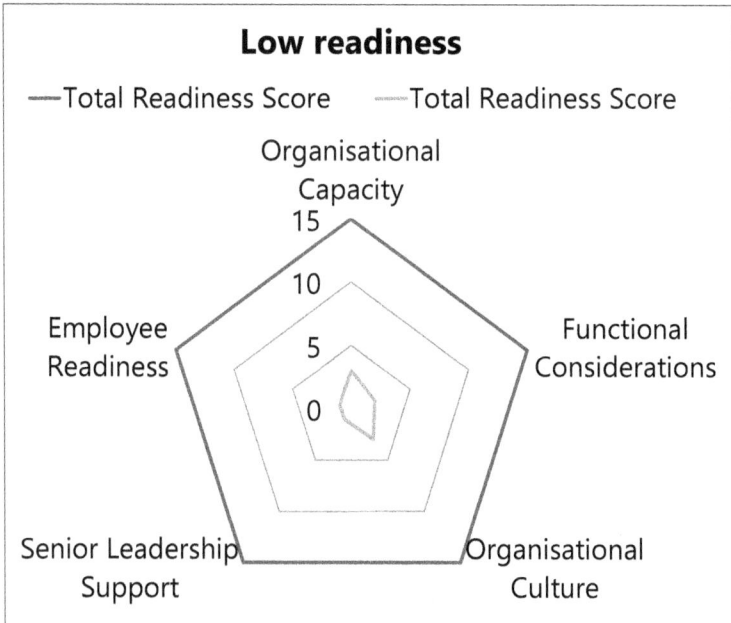

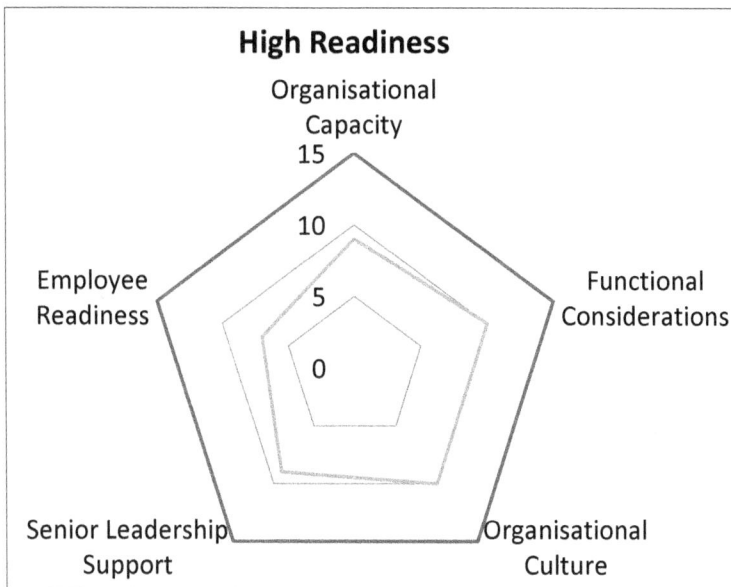

Annexure 2: RACI Matrix

RACI MATRIX: R-Responsible; A-Accountable; C-Consulted; I-Informed

You can use the RACI matrix below to present roles and responsibilities to stakeholders, as it provides information on each role player's responsibilities in the different stages of the process.

SUCCESSION PROCESS	SUCCESSION CHAMPION	EXECUTIVE	GENERAL MANAGERS	HR PRACTITIONER	MANAGERS
Develops the strategy, process and measures to implement the succession management strategy	R	A	C	I	I
Ensures implementation of the succession strategy and succession process	I	I	A	R	C
Embeds integrated succession management in business	I	I	A	C	C
Quarterly talk about talent conversations are held	R	A	A	R	I
Development of talent pools for key positions	I	A	R	I	C
Validation and confirmation of talent into key positions (post assessment)	R	A	A	I	I
Continuous engagement of talent	I	I	A	C	I
Identification of middle and junior talent for critical roles	I	I	A	R	C
Identify and develop critical skill designate programmes	R	A	C	I	I
Monitor and report on succession analytics, progress and statistics	A	I	C	R	C

Annexure 3: Change and communication plan

	Target Audience	Communication Objective	Message	Key Communication Channel	Responsible Person
Preparing for Change	Executives	To position and get buy-in into the initiative	The importance of succession management as a business driver	Presentation of business case through engagement with stakeholders	Succession SME/ HR Director
	Senior Managers	To create awareness of the importance of succession management in the organisation	Succession is a business imperative and needs to be supported by all the managers	Memorandum or email	CEO (Best drafted by HR custodian)
	Executives	To share the implementation plan with deadline dates and get approval	Sharing the succession implementation plan	Presentation	Succession SME
Managing for Change	Line Managers	To invite Line Managers to a training session	Reference the CEO's email and then invite Line Managers to a training session	Email	Succession SME
	Line Managers	To create a common understanding and mind-set about succession	All relevant succession concepts, templates and processes are discussed	Training session	Succession SME

	Target Audience	Communication Objective	Message	Key Communication Channel	Responsible Person
	Line Managers	To trigger the succession process	Mobilises the managers to start the succession process by reinforcing the importance of succession	Management meetings	Senior Manager
	Line Managers	To ensure that the process is completed in contracted timeframes	Communicates available support to managers throughout the succession process and reminds them of deadline dates	Email	HR Manager
	Line Managers	To invite the managers to a succession review session	Recognises managers' commitment to the process and invites them to the session	Calendar invite	General Manager
	Line Managers	To prepare Line Managers for the session by sharing the agenda and the preparation that needs to happen	Provides the agenda and tips for an effective succession review session	Email	HR Manager
	Line Managers	Sends all completed documentation for verification and sign-off to all the managers	Succession templates are sent through with a list of high potential employees	Email with password protected attachment	HR Manager

	Target Audience	Communication Objective	Message	Key Communication Channel	Responsible Person
	Employees	To schedule one-on-one feedback post the succession review session	Provide general development feedback to all employees and communicate to successors the way forward	One-on-one feedback to employees	Line Manager
	Nominated Successors	To schedule an assessment session with successor	Contextualise the assessment by referring to the succession review and manager feedback	Email	Assessment Manager
	Line Managers	To provide assessment feedback on all nominated successors	Provide individual assessment results and identify development areas and group development trends	Presentation of succession results	Assessment Manager
	Senior Manager and Executives	To confirm the final succession plan	To confirm the successors in the succession plan and provide a baseline succession metric on succession coverage	Presentation	Succession SME

	Target Audience	Communication Objective	Message	Key Communication Channel	Responsible Person
	Confirmed Successors	To provide individual assessment feedback	Individual assessment feedback and crafting of development plan	One-on-one feedback with employees	Assessment Manager
	Line Manager	To discuss the development plan	Share the draft development plan and discuss further manager input	One-on-one meeting	Confirmed Successor
Reinforcing Change	Line Managers	To talk about talent succession on a quarterly basis	Schedule this session with all Line Managers to discuss successor progress	Discussion forum	Succession SME

Annexure 4: Training outcomes

Training outcomes	Reasons info should be covered
Key succession concepts	There is common language in the organisation about how the succession concepts should be used.
Philosophy and principles of talent in the organisation	Provides the context and rules of engagement.
The list of critical roles in the organisation	Line Managers understand what roles are considered critical in the organisation which focuses the discussion.
Succession process templates	Managers learn how to complete these templates in the correct way. They understand why certain information is included and why it is important.
Manager roles and responsibilities	Explain the role of Line Managers throughout the process.
Career conversation simulation	Provide skills to managers for having tough career conversations.
Managing resistance	There will be different forms of resistance during this process. Provide techniques to manage this.
Succession review simulation	Incorporate an actual succession review with dummy case studies and ask managers to role play a succession review.
Development identification scenario	Provide the same case studies used in the succession review to identify suitable development interventions.

Annexure 5: Executive letter to management team

Dear Colleague

There are numerous strategic projects on the horizon, which require an in-depth understanding of our people's bench strength for succession into future leadership roles in the business units. Succession management is the process of identifying high-potential employees, evaluating and honing their skills and abilities, and preparing them for advancement into senior positions which are key to the success of business operations and objectives.

Succession management is critical for the following reasons:

To avoid extended and costly vacancies in key positions and to ensure the stability of business operations.

To provide meaningful developmental opportunities for both the organisation and its employees.

To help develop a diverse workforce by enabling decision makers to look at the future demographic representation in the business unit as a whole.

To this end, please accept the invitation to attend a forum where our HR Business Partner, **name of HR manager**, will orient us into our succession management policy and processes. We will be briefed on the succession template, key terminology, and the actions we need to take.

Please note that I will set up a follow-up succession session in your diary, at which time we will discuss your input into the succession plan for **name of business department**. At this session we will review your direct reports and assess their suitability for succession.

Annexure 6: Senior manager email to managers

Dear (Insert employee name)

The implementation of career management at the operational level is a key strategic deliverable in 2018.   You are core to our business, hence it is important to engage with you on your career expectations. This information will assist in identifying critical information such as your career mobility and aspirations in the organisation. Your own career goals and aspirations form an integral part of the organisation's succession and developmental planning process.

All that is expected of you is the following:

Complete **the attached career questionnaire.** This forms part of your preparation for the career discussion. Please complete your career discussion questionnaire before our meeting.
Next you need to complete the required fields in **the talent form.** There is an example that will help you complete this form.
Set up a time in my diary to have a discussion with me once you have completed the documents before the end of ....(Provide deadline date).

I look forward to supporting you through this process.

Kind regards,

Annexure 7: Career questions

1. What are your short term (next 2 years) and long term (next 3 to 5 years) career goals?

2. In meeting these career aspirations, what would be the next position you would be interested in pursuing in the organisation?

3. What have you done thus far or what plans do you have in place to obtain this next position you are interested in?

4. Considering your work background and experiences, what do you feel are your strongest personal attributes, skills, knowledge and abilities? List three strengths.

5. Are there any aspects of your competence or experience that you feel are in need of further development for your future role, or are there competencies (knowledge, skills and abilities) you would like to develop? List three development gaps.

6. Are you presently mobile and willing and able to relocate for future career positions?

Annexure 8: High potential indicators (Line Manager completes)

	Examples of Potential Indicators for Succession	
	Please indicate yes, no or sometimes	
1	Judgement	Does the employee have a track record of showing effective judgement when making decisions?
2	EQ	Does this employee demonstrate emotional resilience when they are faced with difficult situations?
3	Performance track record	Does the employee continuously meet performance objectives and have a great performance record?
4	Energy	Does the employee demonstrate passion and drive for results?
5	Continuous learning	Does the employee actively seek opportunities to continuously improve their knowledge, skills and experience?
6	Accountability	Does the employee take ownership by identifying causes of challenges and resolving these?
7	Initiative	Does the employee use their own initiative, energy and drive to create and respond to opportunities or situations in order to make things happen?
8	Agility	Is the employee able to adapt to changing demands of projects with ease?
9	Leadership	Does the employee demonstrate strong leadership skills?
10	Engagement	Does the employee demonstrate commitment in their role and are they engaged with the organisation?

Annexure 9: Talent profile example

You can include the Talent Grid in this form if your organisation uses it.

TALENT PROFILE

Name			Job title	
Department			Reports to	
Gender			Business unit	
Race			Age	
Risk of leaving	Low; Medium; High		Tenure in organisation	
Impact of leaving	Low; Medium; High		Time in position	
Performance rating	2017	2018	Total direct reports	

Professional Associations		Qualifications	Date	Mobility
1		1		Within region
2		2		Within South Africa
3		3		Globally

Core Strengths		Areas of Development	
1		1	
2		2	
3		3	

Short Term Career Aspirations (Next 2 Years)	Long Term Career Aspirations (Next 3-5 Years)
Immediate Development Actions	Long Term Development Actions
Short Term Career Path	Long Term Career Path

Emergency Cover	Ready Now	Ready 1 - 2 Years
Overall Comments		

Line Manager to complete these fields	Employee to complete this information

Annexure 10: Succession template

	Position of critical role	Name of Incumbent	Length in Position	Age	Division	Emergency Cover	Job Title	Race	Gender	Ready Now	Job title	Race	Gender	Ready 1-2 YEARS	Job Title	Race	Gender	Ready 2-3 YEARS	Job title	Race	Gender
e.g.	Financial Manager	Peter Pan	15 Years	55 years	Finance	None available	Financial Accountant	Not applicable	Not applicable	Tony Stark	Credit Manager	White	Male	Clark Kent	Management accountant	Coloured	Male	None available		Not applicable	Not applicable
1																					
2																					
3																					
4																					
5																					
6																					
7																					
8																					
9																					
10																					

Annexure 11: Succession status visual map

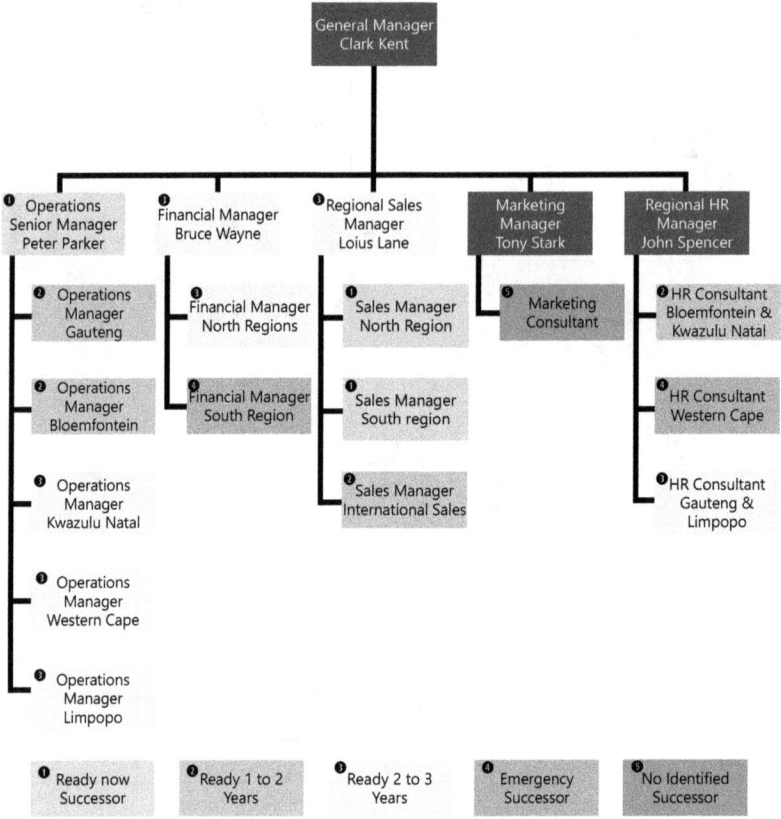

Annexure 12: Ongoing leadership messages

Talent messages from leadership for communicating executive support	Rationale
We acknowledge the significant contribution of all our employees.	We will be able to engage our employees and validate their contribution. We will rejuvenate a disengaged workforce.
We strive to provide continuous and honest feedback for the purposes of growth.	Inculcate a culture of senior people giving proper feedback from a recruitment perspective.
We evaluate people objectively and holistically looking at their engagement, aspiration and abilities.	These are three elements of the talent definition. We need to move away from only focusing on functional competence.
We will develop our employees for future growth and create a learning culture.	We need to shift the culture to employees taking ownership for careers, and provide resources for development.
Every senior appointment must be dealt with transparency, fairness and objectivity.	Build trust and credibility in the way senior appointments are made.
We commit to doing the talent management process on an annual basis.	Build sustainability in the process and embed thinking in the culture.
We will foster an organisational culture that breeds excellence.	Create a high performance culture, create industry experts.
Focus on the measurement of talent tracking in the organisation.	Measure the efficiency of our processes. What gets measured gets done.

Annexure 13: Feedback Form

FEEDBACK GATHERING WORKSHEET

Rank the following statements

1 = strongly disagree, 2 = disagree, 3 = not sure, 4 = agree, 5 = strongly agree

a) I understand the business rationale for the succession management

1	2	3	4	5

b) I have been adequately trained on the succession management process

1	2	3	4	5

c) I understand and can apply the high potential criteria in selecting successors

1	2	3	4	5

d) I have the necessary skills to implement succession management in my business

1	2	3	4	5

e) I understand how to complete all the succession templates

1	2	3	4	5

f) I have the necessary skills to have career discussions with employees

1	2	3	4	5

g) I am aware of the different biases when selecting successors

1	2	3	4	5

h) The succession management process was effectively implemented in the business

1	2	3	4	5

i) I am committed to identifying stretch development opportunities for my successors

1	2	3	4	5

j) I am committed to championing the succession management process in the organisation

Recommended Readings

Erker, S., Smith, A., Paese, M. & Concelman, J. 2013. *6 Talent Strategy Levers for a Vuca World*. [Online] Available at: https://www.ddiworld.com/blog/tmi/october-2013/6-talent-strategy-levers-for-a-vuca-world [Accessed 14 February 2018].

Recommended Websites

CEO Succession: Why It Pays to Have a Plan: https://www.youtube.com/watch?v=pM3CbxYwcRQ

Why Succession Planning is essential: The Case of the Runaway Talent: https://www.youtube.com/watch?v=GZ8C3ie0drw

Succession Development: https://www.youtube.com/watch?v=KNt7Eri05iE

David Ulrich on Succession Planning: https://www.youtube.com/watch?v=ej8qGWMYgys

Using the Nine Box for Succession Planning - A 3-Minute Crash Course: https://www.youtube.com/watch?v=YmbFWTC62wU

Identifying Leaders with the Performance Potential Matrix: https://www.youtube.com/watch?v=tM1FaZoktaQ

70/20/10 Development Plans: https://www.youtube.com/watch?v=80lm4REbPCw

References

Business Families Foundation. 2014. *Succession Planning Quotes.* [Online] Available at: https://businessfamilies.org/read/tag/succession-planning/ [Accessed 26 October 2017].

CEB. n.d. *Succession Management. Four Reasons why your succession plan will fail.* [Online] Available at: https://www.cebglobal.com/human-resources/smb-hr/succession-management.html [Accessed 20 October 2017].

Charan, R., Drotter, S. & Noel, J. 2001. *The Leadership Pipeline.* San Francisco: John Wiley and Sons.

Corporate Leadership Council. 2011. *High Impact Succession Management: An overview of CLC Human Resources Best Practice Research.* [Online] Available at: https://www.slideshare.net/AshokPrabhakar79/succession-planning-24329771 [Accessed 28 November 2017].

George, M.D.E. 2013. *Business Capability Maturity Model – Simplified.* [Online] Available at: http://managewithoutthem.com/2013/03/04/business-capability-maturity-model-simplified/ [Accessed 16 November 2017].

Heshmat, S. 2015. *What is confirmation bias? Wishful thinking.* [Online] Available at: https://www.psychologytoday.com/blog/science-choice/201504/what-is-confirmation-bias [Accessed 05 October 2017].

Hiatt, J.M. & Creasey, T.J. 2003. *Change Management.* Colorado: Prosci Research.

Lamoureux, K., Campbell, M. & Smith, R. 2009. *High-Impact Succession Management: Executive Summary.* [Online] Available at: https://files.eric.ed.gov/fulltext/ED507599.pdf [Accessed 14 February 2018].

Lanier, M. 2012. *Organisational Culture: Are you taking it to the next level?* [Online] Available at: https://hroutsider.wordpress.com/2012/04/09/organizational-culture-are-you-taking-it-to-the-next-level/ [Accessed 5 September 2017].

Michaels, E., Hanfield-Jones, H. & Axelrod, B. 2001. *The War For Talent.* Boston, MA: Harvard Business Press.

Psychologenie. n.d. *Did You Know the Amazing Psychology Behind the Bandwagon Effect?* [Online] Available at: https://psychologenie.com/psychology-behind-bandwagon-effect [Accessed 20 September 2017].

Quotes Gram. n.d. *Succession planning quotes.* [Online] Available at: http://quotesgram.com/succession-planning-quotes/ [Accessed 28 September 2017]

Rassi, E. n.d. *6 quotes about the value of succession planning from 2005.* [Online] Available at: http://www.halogensoftware.com/blog/6-quotes-about-the-value-of-succession-planning- from-2015 [Accessed 30 December 2015].

Talent Management & TBHRM. 2009. *Succession Management Maturity.* [Online] Available at: https://agis93.wordpress.com/2009/11/25/bersin-succession-management-maturity/ [Accessed 5 September 2017].

World Health Organisation. 2017. *Frequently Asked Questions.* [Online] Available at: http://www.who.int/suggestions/faq/en/ [Accessed 15 September 2017].

End Notes

1   Michaels, Hanfield-Jones & Axelrod, 2001, p. 4.
2   Charan, Drotter & Noel, 2002, p. 4.
3   Quotes Gram, n.d., p. 10.
4   Rassi, 2015, p. 21.
5   Business Families Foundation, 2014, p. 21.
6   CEB, n.d., p. 25.
7   George, 2013, p. 28.
8   Lanier, 2012, p. 28.
9   Talent Management & TBHRM, 2009, p. 33.
10   Lamoureux, Campbell & Smith, 2009.
11   World Health Organisation, 2017, p. 35.
12   Heshmat, 2015, p. 61.
13   Psychologenie, n.d., p. 62–63.
14   Corporate Leadership Council, 2011, p. 73.
15   Hiatt & Creasey, 2003, p. 74.

Index